SUMMIT 74

The Canada/Russia Hockey Series

Dick Beddoes and John Roberts

METHUEN

Toronto · London · Sydney · Wellington

ISBN 0458-91170-4

Cover photo courtesy *Sports International*.
Black and white photos courtesy Canadian Press

Printed and bound in Canada

1 2 3 4 5 6 WO-74 9 8 7 6 5 4

PREFACE

Where were you in '72 when Paul Henderson scored with 36 seconds remaining to win the Kremlin Kup or the Campbell Cup in the series Canada couldn't lose. The series that we couldn't be beaten in even one game. The series that they weren't even going to score a goal against us.

If our friends in Ottawa had taken a poll the afternoon of the final game of the absenteeism from work across Canada, the figures would doubtless have been astonishing. Those who had a television or access to one were in front of the tube in their homes, in the local pub, or in the office, watching "the hockey series of the century." Rental TV's were more precious than gold, and harder to get. And those who didn't have a box likely went out and lifted one.

When Henderson scored the country went nuts. Every saloon in the country went nuts. The Halifax riots had nothing on this one. Send Harry Sinden the bill. We won, by the skin of our chauvinism, but we won. Forget our predictions; with a country-wide sigh of relief Henny became a national hero. He could have appointed himself king on that day and no one would have said a word.

Where are you in '74, when the likes of Ricky Ley (remember him, from the Leafs?), Don McLeod of Houston, Gordie, Mark and Marty Howe of TV commercial fame, and assorted other World Hockey Association mercenaries take to the ice in an attempt to retain our national honour? If we lose . . . well, it's not the NHL. We could have sent better. If we win . . . we're still the champs, the Great Ones, and our national game and our national pride and our national egos will have been gratified. The flag will remain high on Parliament Hill, old women and children will still be safe, and Hockey Night in Canada will be true to its word. IF we win.

The economy may be falling down around our ears and our pocketbooks, the cold war may be very hot in some parts of the world, and the WHA *may be* second-rate (although you'd never know it to listen to Bill Hunter), but damn it, it does really matter whether or not we win this series. To hell with Egypt and Cyprus and the whole lot of them. The only action that really counts now is in Quebec City and Toronto and Winnipeg and Vancouver, and later in downtown Russia.

So, win or lose, this book is dedicated to Team Canada 74. It's the story of their battle against the Soviet powerhouse that shook our very culture when they nearly pulled it off in '72. Forget the NHL and the WHA; this is Team Canada—not merely Team Canada 74, but the representatives of our national game, and indeed our country. We share in their success or failure.

Dick Beddoes is a sports reporter and columnist with the Toronto *Globe and Mail*. John Roberts the General Editor of the Methuen Sports Series.

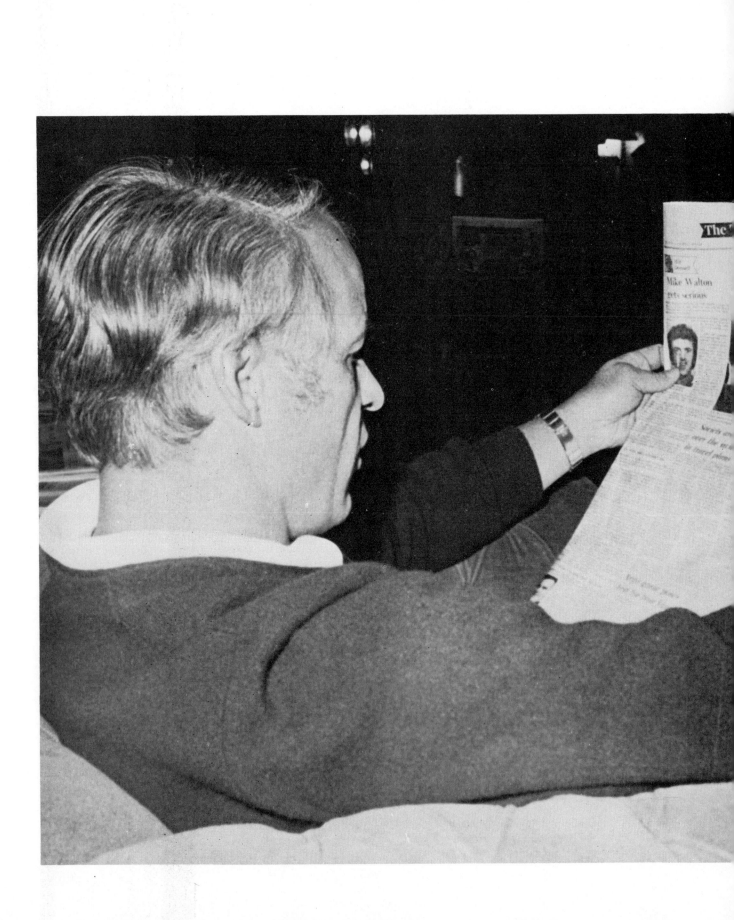

INTRODUCTION

1972

Sports writers reached for superlatives as they strained to fence in a story with exclamation marks!!!! And there seemed no adequate way to tell it. The art of fiction, even on sports pages, was dead. Reality had strangled invention. Only the utterly preposterous, the inexpressibly fantastic, would ever seem plausible again.

Perhaps the best way to tell it is with a half-boob air, aware, as adults should be, that when all is said and done, hockey is a game that small boys play, whether in Montreal or in Minsk. Thus, on the cool dark Moscow night of September 28, 1972, a Thursday: The large Red Square became an embarrassed White Flag waving acceptance of defeat, *pro tem*; The handle of the Hammer broke and the Sickle was a rusty old jacknife; The Lenin Mausoleum trembled as though Richard Nixon was selling used cars in the Kremlin courtyard; All the vodka turned sour in the Russian vats; The Politburo disintegrated and 55 years of Communist rule became just another 5-Year Plan; The garlic went rancid in the Ukrainian sausage, and the cops in the KGB couldn't find the floor if they fell out of bed; Pravda was nothing more than a soggy Soviet throwaway, and Lennie Brezhnev's blood turned to cold beet borscht. All because Team Canada 72 —alias Team NHL or the Eagleson Athletic Club or Team Ugly—won a cozy little series at the summit in the last 34 seconds of the last game in the most discussed, most cussed tournament in hockey history.

The score was tied 5-5 and the eight-game series was snarled: three for Canada, three for the Soviet Union, one tied. A tie in the last game would have been eminently satisfying, even to the most chauvanistic Canadian fanatic. Then, in the last minute, play boiled around Russian goalkeeper Vladislav Tretiak. Phil Esposito, refusing to leave the ice on a line change, controlled the puck out of a chaotic scramble.

"Somebody shot it into the Russian zone," Esposito explained later. "I whacked it toward the net. The goalie made a save, but here came Henny and he tucked it into the net."

Henny—Paul Garnet Henderson—sprang approximately nine feet into the air, then landed in a heap of jubilant teammates. The twilight of civilization had been momentarily averted. Canadians in Moscow's bright Luzhnicki Arena, some 2700 strong, behaved as though they had won a world war. We have, in fact, never sent so many Canadians overseas in one mob outside of a world war. The Canadian zealots were on an emotional treadmill for the duration of their 10-day mission to Moscow, gripped in a tourniquet of tension. Few ever sang *O Canada* so loudly or so passionately off key. Staid Muscovites were startled by the noisily defiant chant, "Go, Canada, Go! Go, Canada, Go!" They were also insulted by another raunchy, inventive battle cry: "Da, Da, Can-a-da! Nyet, Nyet, Sov-i-et! Da, Da, Can-a-da! Nyet, Nyet, Sov-i-et!"

Henderson's goal gratified the chauvinists who had travelled from Canada to Moscow in the biggest airlift since the relief of blockaded Berlin in 1948.

"By God, the Canada goose ain't a dead duck, not yet, anyway. Let's get smashed."

"When I scored that final goal," Henderson would say, "I finally knew what democracy is all about."

That seemed to be slicing the old salami a trifle thick, even Soviet salami. Its true that Henderson's winning goal in the Super Bowlski

conferred upon the country a sense of exciting achievement in the one great game that inflates our national ego. But, cooling off from a satiating orgasmic experience, an observer could reflect on William Buckley's comment on the nature of games.

"If you win a basketball game 50-30 or a hockey game 7-3," Buckley wrote, "you are the better team. If you win by a single point, 6-5, what you have is two evenly matched teams, one of which is lucky."

Henderson, a fleet left wing who knocked down roughly $80,000 yearly from the Toronto Maple Leafs before jumping to the Toronto Toros of the World Hockey Association, scored the winning goal for Team 72 in each of the last three games, and it is reasonable for him to quote Budd Schulberg in rebuttal of Buckley.

"Luck," Schulberg wrote, "is only a bulb that shines when the current is on."

Henderson was turned on as never before in his big-league career, allied with his Toronto associate, Ron Ellis, and Bob Clarke of the Philadelphia Flyers, on the most consistent Canadian forward line. Other Canadian representatives have rarely played better, and may never reach such patriotic peaks again. Few hockey experts believed that big Bill White of the Chicago Black Hawks or solid Gary Bergman, then employed by the Detroit Red Wings, could reach inside themselves and play as efficiently on defence. Most

of all, athletically, the first summit series certified rangy, moose-tall Phil Esposito as a superstar. He could always score, winning five of the previous six scoring titles in the NHL. But in Boston he operated in the shadow of a prodigy, Bobby Orr. Earlier in Chicago he had passed the pucks which Bobby Hull's celebrated slapshot converted into goals.

Orr was injured and couldn't play against Russia in 1972. Hull abandoned the NHL for the Winnipeg Jets of the rival WHA and was barred from playing in the series by spiteful pygmies in the NHL Establishment. Esposito strode into the vacuum created by the absence of Orr and Esposito and, trying harder, No. 2 became No. 1. He played 30 or 35 minutes of every game against the borscht belters—scoring goals (7), setting-up goals (6), forechecking, killing penalties, working on the power play, arguing. He had been put down by a few directors of Hockey Canada as a "moneygrubber" and "unpatriotic" when he demanded certain guarantees in the event of injury. In Stockholm, however, when the Canadians struggled in disarray, Esposito took charge in the dressing room.

"Anybody that doesn't want to stand up for Canada," he declared, "better take off their uniforms and go home. We don't want any quitters on this club."

Four did quit after Team 72 arrived in Moscow. Vic

Hadfield of the New York Rangers, Jocelyn Guevremont of the Vancouver Canucks, and Richard Martin and Gil Perrault of the Buffalo Sabres deserted after coach Harry Sinden didn't pick them to play against Russia. The defections, more than any other factor, seemed to cement the remaining players as a team. Peter Mahovlich, the younger and bigger of the two Mahovlich brothers on the team, muttered a statement to reporters after the last game.

"Don't forget to mention those guys who deserted us," he said. "I'd like to see them take a shot at me when the NHL season begins. What the hell—we became a team when they left."

It was a pistol-paced sports story, with the bladed tension of Jean-Paul Parise's hockey stick poised menacingly above the haircut of a German referee, Joseph Kompalla. But many in the Canadian contingent, Alan Eagleson prominent among them, regarded the confrontation as more than a hockey showdown. Most of them regarded it as Us versus Them, White Hats against Black Hats, Good Guys defying Bad Guys. The older Mahovlich, Frank, devoutly insisted the series was more than a clash between cultures. To the Big M, it became almost a paranoic crusade of Right battling to subdue might.

Mahovlich is the most sensitive of athletes, a prodigy with the puck on his big nights for the Toronto Maple Leafs, Detroit Red Wings, and Montreal

Canadiens, sometimes unable to cope with the barbs and shafts of criticism. During Punch Imlach's abrasive coaching regime in Toronto, Mahovlich suffered two emotional collapses. In Moscow, he seemed to have the impression that a Communist bogeyman lurked under every bed. That may have been right, John Shaw of *Time* magazine's Moscow bureau said, except for the location.

"If the Commies have a bogeyman anywhere in your flat," Shaw said, "its likely to be in the form of an electronic bug in the light fixtures, or the ashtray, or the picture on the wall."

The Canadian players were in the Intourist Hotel, a new Soviet flophouse colloquially called the Moscow Hilton. Intourist, the Soviet travel agency, somehow managed to billet every Canadian yahoo with the players in the Intourist. On the night that the players arrived from Stockholm, the Intourist lobby was jammed with the sort of shoving, shouting, idiotic buffoons who annually turn the Grey Cup celebration into a Grand National Drunk.

Mahovlich was appalled by the rooming arrangements, in spite of the presence of his attractive wife, Marie.

"Look," he said earnestly, "I'm a professional. I'm used to getting up in the morning and practicing hockey, which is my business. This nonsense of noisy fans around upsets me."

Mahovlich had his own

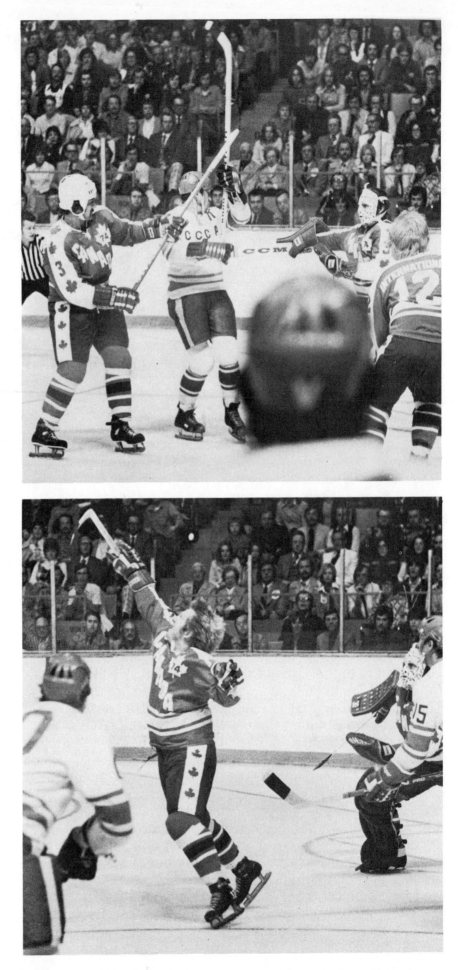

notion of where Team Canada should have been sheltered.

"I'd have preferred to have us players put up in tents alone outside Moscow somewhere, and come in by bus for the games."

His preoccupation with the Moscow menace was reflected in Mahovlich's play. He was benched for two of the eight games with niggling injuries and, in sum, contributed one goal and one assist. The menace absorbed others such as Eagleson, the nimble Toronto lawyer who directs the NHL Players Association.

"The Russians have only one system," Eagleson testified, "and that's the muscle system. I'd rather be a bum in Toronto than a major-general in Russia."

Many Canadian fans and commentators were indignantly convinced that Eagleson acted like a bum in Moscow 72.

"He's a diplomatic disaster," John Robertson wrote in the *Montreal Star* after Eagleson hassled Russian policemen, and was hassled by them, in the last game.

Eagleson vocally protested that a Soviet goal judge did not turn on the red light for the fifth and tying Canadian goal, scored by Yvon Cournoyer. To lend force to his protest, Pal Al rushed from his seat toward the bench occupied by the official scorekeeper. In its long quest for world peace, Russia has always stuck to its guns—even in hockey arenas. Thus, surrounded by Russian guards as he ranted, Eagleson almost

had his right arm wrenched from its socket. He was rescued by several Canadian players who piled over the boards, led by Peter Mahovlich. Skidding across the ice toward the Canadian bench, surrounded by Canadian players, Eagleson lifted the long finger on his right hand in the universal gesture which indicated that the jeering Russians should go commit an indecency against themselves.

"What I was really doing," Eagleson said, "was putting up my thumb in a thumbs-up gesture to the Canadian fans. Films of the game prove this to be so."

Eagleson's ceaseless sticking and moving on behalf of the players union has earned him the respect of most NHL mercenaries. Since 1967 he has bargained for pension benefits and salary increases which the athletes, at an average salary exceeding $50,000 a year, have ample reason to appreciate. In Eagleson's defence, it is worth mentioning that his unremitting scorn for the Russians probably welded Team 72 into a clubby attitude of mean-spirited myopia that shrunk their world in Moscow to the confines of the rink and welcomed few outsiders. His personal bonfire ignited just enough Canadian players to inspire them to barely win. There is no defence, however, to account for Canadian sportsmanship that usually didn't rise any higher than a snail's spoon. Its difficult to endorse Eagleson telling a

Russian interpreter, after the incident of the goal-light-that-didn't-flash, "You're a liar when you tell me the goal light was burned out! You Russians are all a bunch of liars!"

This is how a vest-pocket war, in the autumn of 1972, affected normally rational Canadians. The malady lingers on, but it cannot obscure one vivid cameo after Paul Henderson scored the winning goal. One good Russian player, the chippy Boris Mikhailov, turned away from the jubilant Canadians and skated toward the depressed Soviet bench. The number on the back of his jersey looked huge. No. 13.

July 31, 1974

The mugs were so freshly-hatched from the kiln that they were warm, with no time for proof-reading. At the press conference announcing Team Canada 74 the mugs were a souvenir, a garish sort of geegaw you might win if some guy doesn't guess your weight in a cheap sideshow at the Canadian National Exhibition. It was a rush job with no time for refinement, perhaps an ill omen for the World Hockey Association's semi-summit against the Soviet Union.

The inscription on the mugs was supposed to read TEAM CANADA L'EQUIPE 74. Even on the infamous one-way street of Quebec's queer language bill, *equipe* is the French equivalent of *team*. On the WHA mugs, however, L'EQUIPE (the team) came out L'EQUITE. One hoped, six weeks before the series began, that L'EQUITE did not mean "the quitters."

Quitting is the last thing Wild William Hunter does, particularly when he has a microphone clamped solidly in his bicuspids. Mr. Hunter generally managed Team 74, and helped coach it, and counted the gate receipts, and played head trumpet in the cheerleading, and advised Lennie Brezhnev on international affairs. Mr. Hunter's advice on international affairs is to have one and, when in doubt, punt. He apprenticed to be the Alan Eagleson of Team 74 by more or less running hockey teams in Medicine Hat, Regina, Saskatoon, Blairmore, Yorkton, Moose Jaw, Otter Haunch, Flat Tire, Edmonton and other lovely prairie boondocks.

Mr. Hunter's voice changed when he was five years old. It changed from sporadic to steady, as he proved when he stood up in the Royal York Hotel in Toronto to introduce Team 74. The only impediment in Wild Will's speech was when he paused for breath. Once. Every introductee received a florid fanfaronade as before the Battle of Armageddon, or the Charge of the Light Brigade, or upon being inducted into the all-time all-world hockey hall of blame.

"One of the great goalies of all time . . . ladies and gents . . . Houston's Don McLeod!"

Don Who walked in, limping, to a couple of indifferent claps.

"We give you Bruce MacGregor, who can excite and ignite! One of the world's truly fastest skaters, Tom Webster! One of the great competitors in the history of the game, Cowboy Johnny McKenzie! The distinguished, hard-nosed, super-toughie, Jim Harrison!"

One awed listener murmured, "Migawd, Howie Morenz must have been a busher. All anybody ever called him was great."

Superlatives spilled off Wild Will's glib tongue, while hyperbole cowered under the dias, cringing and whimpering.

"The most colourful, hard-shooting exciter, Mike Walton! . . . An all-time great superstar, Frank Mahovlich! . . . When the final whistle sounded in 1972, the man who rocked the world with his goals, Paul Henderson! . . . Mr. Clutch and Super Saver, Gerry Cheevers!"

And: "Seven times a 50-goal scorer, the first selection for Team 72, the superstar not allowed to play two years ago, but all Canada's gonna see him this year . . . Bobby Hull! . . . "

And: "We've got all the Howe's, who can't be here today because they're opening a supermarket. . . . Those great prospects, Mark and Marty! . . . And the great one, the Daddy of All The Howes . . . Gordie! . . . "

Hunter's ballyhooed bilge rolled on this hot day in Toronto, adjectival claptrap piled on overblown bafflegab, a spielbinder rampant, tubthumper on the rampage.

"Get out the forks, boys," *The Globe and Mail* murmured the next day. "We've been hit by the fallout from a colossal manure spreader."

Mr. Hunter's customary credo is that balderdash baffles brains, but it was necessary to stand back a pace, on August 1, and shake off the dewy-eyed delirium. Hull would play for the WHA selects, as he should have played in 1972 if the warped characters in the NHL had not blackballed him because he dared jump to the WHA. There has never been a left wing with his supershooting and insouciance, rarely a performer with his sense of public relations. He would charm Europe.

Howe, too, but at 46 it seemed that the grandeur that was Gordie was gone. And the questions: Could Henderson catch lightning and bottle it again, without Bobby Clarke doing the forechecking? Could anyone seriously believe that the defence of Team 74 matched the Bergman and White and Savard and Lapointe of 72?

Cheevers is a money goaltender, but Bernie Parent of the Philadelphia Flyers is the best player at that position on the planet. Team Canada 74 needed Orr and Esposito the way Secretariat needed his legs, the way Anne Murray needs her throat. The NHL stars were not playing because the NHL and WHA are still reaching for each other's tonsils. More's the pity. Balderdash, it appeared on August 1, will not baffle a

Frank Mahovlich (left), a new Toronto Toro, and Paul Henderson, whose goals won the 1972 series, share a joke at the reception after being named to the 1974 squad.

Soviet side shooting with its best.

"Team 74 to lose every game by a converted touchdown," John Robertson rashly forecast in the *Montreal Star.*

Training Camp

On the first day of Team Canada's training camp in Edmonton, the 32-man contingent was surprised to find 4500 eager fans on hand to watch them show their stuff and sweat off their summer baggage in preparation for the impending eight-game series against the Russians and the three game exhibition schedule in Finland, Sweden and Czechoslovakia.

"It's good with the building empty," said coach Billy Harris, "but with the crowd there, it forces them to think of September 17. It also forces them to realize that people are interested in them."

The coach couldn't have picked a better training camp city than Edmonton, Alberta, home of the Edmonton Oil Kings and some of Canada's most rabid hockey fans. As an extra, the team had been offered free accommodation at the Edmonton Plaza Hotel, a newly-opened resting place for the weary and wayward, interested in a little publicity. The hockey rink also came gratis, and no one on the Team Canada executive was heard complaining too loudly.

The team had arrived in supposedly great physical shape. Since the selection of the 1974 dream team on July 31, the players were on the honour system to prepare themselves both physically and mentally for Summit 74—the Big One, the series to end them all (for the WHA, if things didn't go well), the series which would show the world that the WHA was indeed good enough to be in the same rink as the Russians and, by inference, in the same rink as Team Canada 72, and by further inference, in the same rink as the NHL. The inferences were long and tedious, but one fact remained—honour and country were at stake.

There was barely a dry eye in the rink.

"I've been on two Stanley Cup winning teams with the Bruins," gushed everyone's favourite and super patriot Johnny McKenzie, "but I've never experienced anything like this."

While everyone present was wondering what "this" was, Rick Smith, himself an expatriate Bruin, cleared the air.

"I wondered what it would be like when we came together, but this I didn't expect. Guys will go out of their way to do anything for each other."

Oh.

The honour was there, then. But you don't win them all on your honour. Otherwise the Philadelphia

Flyers (to but briefly mention that other league) would have won old Lord Stanley's basin from their inception, and that hadn't happened, except for this year, when the Broad Street Bullies were especially honourable. No matter. We're going to win.

Coach Harris, not one to make idle threats, had warned the team to "arrive ready to play" in Edmonton, and most of them did. Frank Mahovlich daily graced our newspapers with his push-up technique. Bobby Hull, his now-tarnished golden rug just a little ragged around the edges, switched on his afterburners as he flew up and down the ice. They all seemed to be in good shape, with the exception of Rick Ley, who looked a little as if he had recently escaped from some 15¢ donut machine, where he had been held captive over the summer. With lengthy digressions about team co-operation and Canada's honour, coupled with two healthy legs apiece and a pair of skates, they seemed ready.

But a few thousand miles away, on the other side of the pond, their opponents were surely ready. No sixteen days of skating for them before attacking the walls of Quebec City. They were ready, and everyone in Canada who had a brain to think with knew that they were. It was hard to swallow good old Chuckles Kulagin's story that his team had come together on the same day as Team Canada. Visions of year-round

hockey rinks in Siberia flitted through the country's collective mind, of a second team of skaters dressed up in Canadian uniforms to provide the opposition through the long Arctic nights, instructed to throw the occasional body check and spear the odd National to simulate game conditions and stimulate the old adrenelin. No one expected the Soviets to be pushovers, as they had generally been regarded in August of 1972. They were going to be tough. And how tough are we? How will the talent match up? The answers remained hidden before Game 1, but everyone who followed hockey, with the exception of a few nuts with money to bet and burn, must have thought "not good enough." This was only the WHA. No Phil Esposito and company this time.

True, the Jet's here. But nagging little questions seem to pop up whenever he's mentioned. Is he still as good as he was playing for the Black Hawks, or is the WHA talent merely making him look good? After all, he didn't walk away with any scoring title. Gordie and the boys are here, or at least are expected any day. But Gordie's a bit long in the tooth, and the boys a bit short. And you don't score too many with your elbows.

Frank and Paul are here. But Frank didn't do too much in '72. Why should we expect any different now? And Paul . . . well, Paul's okay, and he did score those three game winners back then, but. . . .

Rejean Houle, Bobby Hull and Gerry Cheevers talk it over, possibly about Hull's new hair, at the Team Canada reception in Toronto.

But Our Side came to camp ready. Let's worry about those other things later. "Canada will win five of the eight games against the Soviet Union," predicted Big Bill White at the Shopsy reunion in Toronto.

One had to wonder whether Bill wasn't into his cups just a bit when he made that prediction.

"I'm not joking," he said, hastening to erase a few ill-disguised smirks. I'm convinced Team Canada 1974 will win five games against the Russians for several reasons.

"The key reason is that the players are fully aware of what to expect. Two years ago we didn't know what was in store for us. Secondly, coach Billy Harris has to deal with only 25 players, which is much easier than dealing with 34. Thirdly, Team Canada 74 has more talent than what many might think."

Thanks for the kind words, Bill. Okay, Paul Shmyr and Al Hamilton and Tom Webster and Jim Harrison. The man says that you'll win five. First of all you've got to get through training camp.

Let's retreat a bit, from September 1, when training camp officially opened, to July 30, when the Sunshine Girl was wearing a string bikini and George Gross of the *Toronto Sun* was making educated guesses about Team Canada's starting line-up. The Russians knew who they wanted. On July 29 they had announced their 36-man roster, on the very day that Billy Harris turned 39. Happy birthday, Billy, from your pal Boris. 36 birthday greetings for you from Moscow. Billy agreed to have his birthday photo taken for the *Sun*, but under one condition: " . . . you're not going to ask me anything about the Team Canada 1974 selection."

Okay, Billy. Until tomorrow. One psychological point for the Russians. Score: Russia 1, Canada 0.

August 1 (*Toronto*): Training camp one month today. The press conference was held today to announce the roster. Paul Shmyr had a beard, J. C. Tremblay had a misspelled mug, and

everyone agreed with Pat Stapleton.

"We have more to prove this time," he said, not meaning the we of Team 72. "People look at big names, but hard work can accomplish a great deal."

The question now arises whether or not enough off-ice hard work can get the team into shape for the Edmonton grand opening, and whether 16 days of ice time can get the team in shape for the Russian onslaught. Are five games in the West against junior all-stars (when did *they* start practicing) enough competition? A lot of questions this fine summer morning. Gotta give the Russians another one.
Score: Russia 2, Canada 0.

September 1 (*Edmonton*): Training camp opens today. While other Canadians are killing themselves on the Labour Day highways and by-ways, Team Canada 74 is getting ready to kill itself on the hockey rinks of western Canada. It's worth one just to see them all here. Well, not all, but give them a point anyhow.
Score: Russia 2, Canada 1.

September 2 (*Edmonton*): Tremblay is trimmer and talkative ("The problem is, most people don't think we're going to win . . . but they still expect us to."), Ley is overweight, the Golden

The man who puts it all together. Billy Harris guides his team through a workout in Edmonton.

Jet has a new hair patch, and Gerry Cheevers, expected to play most of the games against the Soviets (possibly because there's no one else) is philosophical.

"In a series like this, you must have poise to win. Any great team that ever won had it."

Billy Harris maintained his usual approach—low key. He feels that Canada can regain some of the prestige lost against the Russians in 1972, but won't make any firm predictions yet. The first exhibition game is in Medicine Hat three nights from now, and Harris is much too busy experimenting with his lines to let us in on who's going to win. But he will refresh our memories on who's in camp.

"Tentatively, I plan to play Andre Lacroix with Gordie and Mark Howe. And I expect to start with Ralph Backstrom between Bruce MacGregor and Paul Henderson."

Jim Harrison will centre Bobby Hull and Tom Webster, with Mike Walton between Frank Mahovlich and Johnny McKenzie.

This is all very interesting, but still page 31 news (or page 2 of the Sports Section, in a corner below women's tennis and rugger) in the major newspapers. And the big game Thursday in Medicine Hat isn't attracting a great deal of attention outside of that fair city. If Our Side loses Thursday against the junior our side, Billy had better get ready to spend long nights on his experimenting.

Funny thing is, some think that the juniors have a chance.

September 3 (*Edmonton*): Bobby Hull is back again. In the scrimmages to date he's been one of the standouts.

"If anyone here needs reminding of what lies ahead, he shouldn't be here," said the Jet. "I don't mind working hard to stay in shape. That's the way it should be."

"Bobby's been just great," said Harris. "But wait till Gordie steps on the ice. He's got to be an inspiration."

That statement must have made Bobby the Jet feel swell.

The estimated 5000 fans who attended the Edmonton Gardens scrimmage this afternoon saw the Winnipeg Jet at his finest. He'd been touted as Canada's hockey ambassador to Europe and our national sweetheart, a man who's going to turn it on to show the NHL that they should have included him in their 1972 line-up, that with him, the Canuck side would have won handily over the Commisars. He is to provide the colour this time, the charisma, the drive.

In practice he was great. But can he lift the team by himself? Even this early into camp things are riling him a bit.

" . . . it bothers me when I see guys dogging it in practice. . . . You know, before you know it, this thing will be all over and it'll be too late then for second guessing."

Perhaps he was referring to the Howe family, who has the team second guessing already. He and the family were supposed to check in last night, but were delayed by a film-shooting venture. Contracts are money, but this is Team Canada. Where are you Gordie? They need you.

Score another one for the Russians. Them 3, Us 1.

September 4 (*Edmonton*): The Great One arrived today, and stepped right into the thick of things, the first time he'd been on skates since the finals of the WHA playoffs last May.

"I had to plead with him to content himself with a skating session in the afternoon after the scrimmage," reported Harris. "He wanted to get into the thick of it right away. I couldn't believe the guy. He was matched with Bobby Hull in the rink-wide skating drill and he was matching him stride for stride."

More inspiration.

"Gordie's going to help us no matter what," insisted Hull, obviously not miffed that Howe was considered to be more inspiration than he was. "Whether he plays 30 minutes a game or five, he'll be an inspiration."

Hopefully inspiration will be enough for now. The players look very, weary after the scrimmages. The Russians announced today that they've sliced their squad to 27 players. But Gordie's here, so who cares. Score: Russia 3, Canada 2.

September 5 (Edmonton): Tucked away into the bottom right hand corner of one of the sports pages of a Toronto newspaper today is a few lines on Vern Buffey's refereeing school. It's running smoothly, Vern tells us, even though the Russians can't speak English, a Finn and a Pole are missing, and Joseph Kompalla isn't.

September 6 (Medicine Hat): Bobby Hull scored three times tonight in Team Canada's first encounter anywhere with anyone except the media, a 7-2 win over a team of Western Canada Junior Hockey League All-Stars. The select's performance was decent enough, but no one in the standing room only crowd of 5115 forgot for a moment that the juniors aren't the Russians. The whole idea of this series against the juniors is to give Team Canada some competition (?) before their Quebec City appearance, and it has to be difficult for our national squad to look bad against a team of rank (!!) amateurs.

It was obvious that Team Canada was glad to get away from the monotony of scrimmages, even though they've only been at it for five days. Paul Shmyr and Marty Howe threw their weight around, and all concerned seemed jovial, even if they had to pick Medicine Hat to be jovial in.

September 7 (Brandon): Team Canada 6, Juniors 5. Frank Mahovlich scored in the last minute to salvage the win. Hmmm.

Gordie, Mark and Marty Howe rest after a practice in Edmonton. A great deal of Team Canada's success rests with these three.

September 8 (Calgary): The newspaper headlines told it all:
TEAM CANADA DROPS GAME AND MAY HAVE LOST HULL
SWEDISH REFEREE ANGERS WALTON, HOWE SLASHES RIVAL AS JUNIORS DEFEAT TEAM CANADA

Our Side looked bad tonight in their third exhibition game against the juniors, so bad, in fact, that the word "bush" would have been kind to use in describing them.

The estimated 8000 in the Calgary Corral were on the juniors' side from the start. By the third period, however, the juniors were the overwhelming choice as Team Canada reverted to backroom tactics to subdue the fired-up kids. At 8:08 of the third, with the juniors leading 2-1, Ley was assessed a penalty. Mike Walton showed a lot of class by heaving his stick and gloves in protest. A short while later, Gordie Howe (yes, Gordie) slashed a junior in frustration. Resentment was building among the fans, and Team Canada's credibility was crumbling. The game ended as an exercise in futility and a reminder that the Russians were a lot closer than some of the players imagined them to be. Team Canada lost, and the excuses weren't far behind.

"We're trying to play for Canada, and this is the way they treat us," said Paul Shmyr, sounding strangely like Phil Esposito in Vancouver two years ago.

"There's no doubt we

12

Gerry Cheevers, who is expected to play goal for most of the series, gets help from Rick Ley and juniors Dennis Sobchuk and Ron Clupperfield.

don't want to lose. . . . But we have to remember what these games are for. We aren't trying to prove we can beat the juniors, but to get in shape," said Rick Smith philosophically.

Harris wouldn't comment directly on the team's poor showing.

"The past three games have been to experiment and to attempt to get them into condition."

They were supposed to be in condition a week ago, Billy.

Bobby Hull hurt his knee in the second period and the extent of his injury isn't known.

"It happens once a year," Bobby told reporters. ". . . I am optimistic. Bad timing. That's all."

To say that his injury came at a bad time is a gross understatement.

Team Canada resembled nothing more than a pack of clowns on skates tonight without Hull, who has scored 5 goals to date. Hull has been the only truly effective Team Canada member, the only one really in shape.

Ominous rumblings about the officiating tonight. Team Canada is concerned about their competence, Vern Buffey about their ability. A bad day all around, and another one for the Soviets. Score: Russia 4, Canada 2.

September 10 (*Saskatoon*): The Golden Jet has survived. He should be back in training camp tomorrow or Thursday. The sun is shining, the flag is flying, the Jet is back. One for us. Score: Russia 4, Canada 3.

September 11 (*Saskatoon*): The Team put it all together tonight and beat the juniors 6-1, with Gordie scoring three. Reports centred not on the play, but on the refereeing. A Swede and a Pole handled this one, and at times their calls had the fans rolling in the aisles with laughter. Words like "ridiculous," "fallible" and "obvious" were used to describe what was missing and what was not. Maybe the fans were laughing, but it's painfully obvious that while Team Canada might be improving, the officiating isn't. The fans won't be laughing if the same thing happens in Quebec City.

September 12 (*Edmonton*): Team Canada spent part of the day golfing. Team Russia competed in an international tournament in Moscow. They're due to arrive in Canada on Sunday. Hull, Bernier and Henderson are slightly injured. Gratton and Harrison have been told to shave off their beards.

Oh, yes. Team Canada 74 beat the juniors 8-0 in their final tune-up before Tuesday's opening match in Quebec City. McKenzie took his turn to score three tonight.

Page 36 of the Toronto *Globe and Mail* had a little something to say about the game.

"It would be difficult to raise hopes for the success of Team Canada from this game, with coach Billy Harris juggling lines."

If Team Canada can win 8-0 and still be considered weak, the Russians must be considered pretty good. Our Side hasn't shown well in the games to date. We haven't even seen the Russians this time around, and already we know they're good because the 74's aren't.

The Soviet side defeated Finland 8-1 and 7-3 this week in the international tournament. Neither Soviet win was against a squad of juniors, but against a national team. In all fairness, it must be admitted that the ranks of the Finnish national team have been depleted by defections to the ranks of the World Hockey Association. But nevertheless the Russians sound good, feel good, act good . . . are good.

It's likely that Joseph

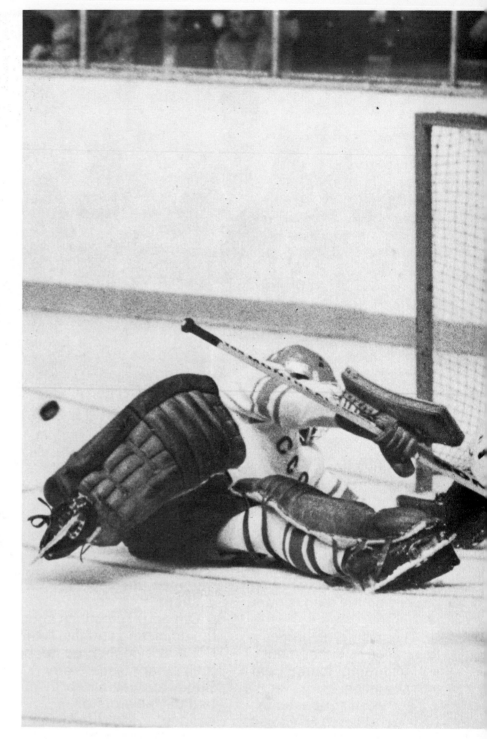

Kompalla of West Germany will work two games in the upcoming eight game series. One more for them.

Final score: Russia 5, Canada 3. The Russians will win the series 5 games to 3. It's questionable where the Canadians will get there three wins from. Maybe they've had them already.

The Russians arrived in Montreal late Saturday night en route to Quebec City, armed with "strategy and technical points" which they had picked up in the 1972 series. Seventeen of the players on the 1974 team were on the '72 squad. Canada has three repeaters.

"We've got some new players on this team, but the team is no weaker than the one in 1972," observed the friendly Russian coach, Boris Kulagin. "We'd like to play as good in this country as we did in 1972 and better hockey than we did in Moscow."

The next day, Howe and Hull witnessed the Soviet practice.

"They're nothing but a bunch of superbly conditioned athletes," Howe stated, tongue-in-cheek. "What strength."

Hull was also impressed. "They're so strong and they can do everything with the puck. I don't know who said they couldn't shoot a puck. They can blister it."

Canadians have to be immensely impressed with the Soviet team, even though they're here to steal our hockey crown which they claim they've got anyhow. The Russians insist that they respect our Team 74, but there's no doubt they feel they can defeat the Canadian squad and avenge the '72 loss.

The night before the first game, Billy Harris sounded as if he was attempting to save his marriage in advance while rationalizing what most are convinced will be a solid drubbing at the hands of the Russians.

"We will try to win all eight games against the Russians," he said. "But if we lose, it won't be the end of the world. My wife and children won't leave me just because we lose. There are more important things in the world than hockey games."

Name one, Billy, just now.

WHA Credibility

It must be said that the 1974 series is being played as much to give credibility to the World Hockey Association as it is for the fun of playing the Russians and retaining Canada's honour in international ice hockey competition.

Team Canada has a superb salesman in bombastic Bill Hunter, part owner of the Edmonton Oilers and general manager of Team Canada. It was he who arranged for the exhibition matches against the juniors, who promoted this team of mostly non-entities and developed public support for them.

But all the press in the world isn't going to put the puck past Vladimir Tretiak. There simply will never be the interest in this series or the fan support enjoyed by Team Canada 72 because it is generally agreed that Team 74, or Team WHA, is

inferior. We don't like to back losers.

Hull and Howe can't carry the team alone. They can't be on the ice all of the time. Those who think that the Canadians will win this series are only hoping; those who thought so in 1972 were sure. Those who are now on Team Canada's bandwagon are ready to jump off at a moment's notice, or a game's loss, whichever comes first.

Game 1 in Quebec City is all-important. If Our Side gets shelled, the players on both sides might as well pack their bags and go home. Fans for the remaining three games in Canada will be scarcer than Argonaught Grey Cups. The team does not have the power that the 72's did to convince the people that they can rebound from a defeat in the first game to win all the borscht and vodka.

Billy Harris has been stressing from the onset that the series is only an exhibition of talent and a chance for cultural exchange. Success, how-ever, would mean "bringing us to a par with the NHL in only two years of existence."

That's not really good enough. Canada wants a winner, especially if they're tagged TEAM CANADA. If it was Team WHA or some other label specifically relating to the WHA, it would be a different story. Canadians could rationalize any losses by saying indeed that this wasn't Canada at play, but merely a second-rate bush league still in diapers.

Team Canada 74 has changed that. But it's still the WHA, no matter how you slice it, and a win in this series will help fill the rinks. It's not really a question of being better than Team 72 if they win, but a question of proving that the WHA is indeed as good as the NHL. So it boils down to WHA against NHL, not Team 72 versus Team 74, or Canada against Russia.

For Bobby Hull, this series offers him a chance to get back at the 1972 Establishment. He should have played, but he was locked out by his defection to the WHA. No one can say that Hull wasn't good enough, but this year Bobby can show them all what they missed.

Henderson and Mahovlich were with Team 72, as was Pat Stapleton. But by being in the WHA, and by being let go by their respective NHL teams without either a court battle or a counter offer large enough to change their minds, can we not assume that the Toronto, Montreal, and Chicago owners felt that these three just couldn't cut the ice any longer in the NHL?

To be realistic, Gordie Howe is an old man as far as hockey players go. He has to be physically old when he plays on the same team as his sons.

These five can provide inspiration, but they can't provide miracles. Hull should play well. Mahovlich may or may not, depending on whether or not he has relieved himself of his

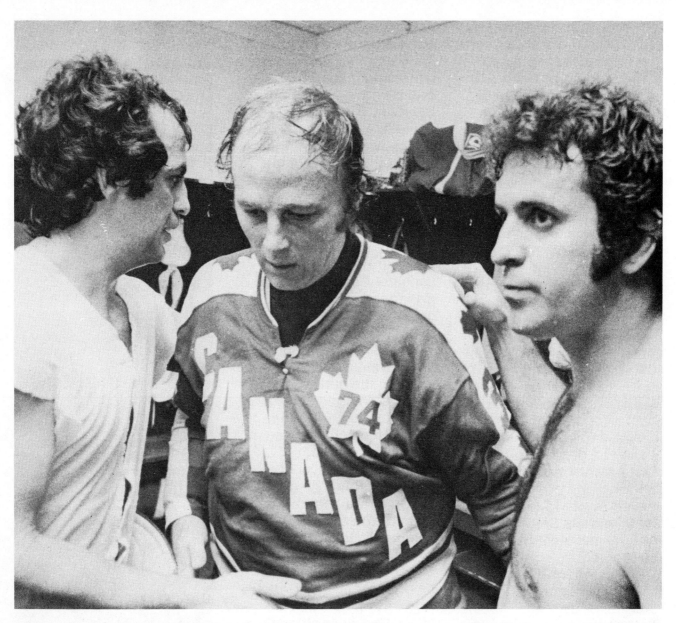

Lacroix, Cheevers, and Walton share a moment after the Toronto game when Cheevers was told that his father-in-law had suffered a heart attack during the game.

mental block against Russians. Henderson had a two mediocre years with the Leafs, and is questionable. It's likely that he should have quit after the '72 series and gone out a winner. Howe won't collapse on the ice, but he may get mighty tired. Stapleton is losing that extra stride. He too should have thought of the pasture in 1972.

Cheevers will have to be superb—even superhuman at times. If he is indeed a money player, now will be the time to throw the rubles into the hat. Most of the NHL rinks will be sold out this year, Kansas City Scouts or not. Without a good showing in this series, which is directly linked to the professionals mentioned, pickings will be impoverished in the WHA rinks this season.

Political Connotations

At a luncheon hosted in the Chateau Frontenac Hotel in Quebec City the day before the opening game of the Canada-Russia hockey series, Federal Health and Welfare Minister Marc Lalonde gave a welcoming speech to the Russians.

"We're behind both teams. We're for peace and friendship."

Now Marc Lalonde, you remember, is the gentle soul who convinced the Toronto Northmen to become the Memphis Southmen in an effort to protect Canadian interests. If he thought that the Russians were coming to Canada for peace and friendship, he might better have protected Canadian interests by meeting the Soviet plane at Montreal and declaring Team Canada the winner of the series on the basis of their snappier sports jackets.

The Russians didn't come to Canada to be peaceful and friendly, Marc. They came to be in hockey games, and if they have to use some of their 1972 tactics to do it, peace and friendship don't mean a thing.

Harris has been playing down the cultural overtones of this series. He doesn't want a cold war on his hands, and properly so. But it can't be denied that when East meets West, especially in view of the power politics played by our friends to the south and the Soviets, cultural implications can't be avoided.

The Russians are playing with a deep sense of national pride. Team Canada is playing as much for the WHA as for Canada. In the patriotism department, the Soviets lead by a mile.

And the 1972 series is not forgotten. Even though Canada won on games, the Russians claim they won on the goal spread, and this is the way the story is told back home. But the players know that they lost, and there's nothing they would like to do more than to score a convincing win over Canada's best this time out.

Coach Boris Kulagin doesn't have much to say about the spirit of co-operation and goodwill the Canuckskis seem to be interested in fostering. He doesn't have to rationalize, though. He knows he's going to win. Instead, Chuckles spoke to reporters in terms of the respect the Soviets have for Team 74. When they win, in Boris' mind, he's going to make sure that the Canadian press corps knows the Russians consider Team WHA Canada's best, that a win over Team 74 will be no different than a win over Team 72, that the Russians are playing Canada's best, and that the entire hockey world is going to know it.

"In Canada, from the World Hockey Association there can be no poor players on the level of a selected team," he panned. Who told him that there might be? He was confident. He almost smiled. Russia would beat Canada. The East would beat the West. The Dark Ice Age was on its way back after a two-year absence.

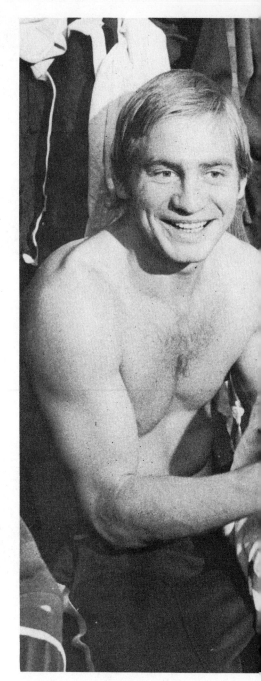

Prelude to the First Game, September 17, in Quebec City

Tension gripped Team 74 before the first game of Super Bowlski Two, the up-tight feeling Montcalm must have had when Wolfe's troops attacked him from the rear that time on the Plains of Abraham, in 1759.

Observers detected what they thought was the flatness that goes with fear —the flatness of losing.

"Against these guys," Bobby Hull would say of the favoured Russians, "we can't afford to psych ourselves out. I hope that doesn't happen to Big Frank."

Hull meant Frank Mahovlich, one of three Team Canadians back for a replay against Boris Kulagin's Kremlin Crowd. The others were Pat

The Russians are here. Bodunov and Yakushev relax after a practice session.

Stapleton and Paul Henderson.

Gordie Howe, who has known hockey pressure for 26 years without sprouting an ulcer, said, "It's no use worrying about the Russians the way that Frank does. You could get sick that way."

Many in the Canadian contingent of 1972 regarded the first summit series as more than a mere hockey showdown. It was Culture versus Culture, Bad versus Good. In 1974 Billy Harris played down any such ideological conflicts. The coach of Team Canada kept saying, as though to remind himself, "The only sane way to view this series is that it's supposed to be eight friendly games. All our forecast is that we won't lose the first game 7-3, the way the first Team Canada did."

Two years previously, Mahovlich had devoutly insisted that the series was more than a contest between cultures. To the Big M, it became a paranoic crusade of Right battling to subdue Might. Two years ago, I recall, Mahov's attitude was caught in cameo in Maple Leaf Gardens on the morning before the second game. The Soviet Selects had won the first game on a shocking Saturday night in Montreal, and incredulous witnesses were aghast to hear themselves babbling wild improbabilities about a World Serious without a single Canadian victory.

That morning the Federal leader of the Progressive Conservatives, Robert Stanfield, arrived in the Gardens with a publicity flack. Stanfield posed on the ice with the hearty president of the Gardens, Harold Ballard, who fitted the Tory chief into a Team Canada jersey. Mahovlich, standing near the boards and smoking a furious cigar, watched Stanfield pose.

"Damn politicians," he grumbled. "Always climbing on the bandwagon as though this is just a game. Don't they know this is war?"

The Canadians won the second game then, 4-1, perhaps one of the most exciting ever played in the Gardens.

The following day, a Tuesday, they travelled from Toronto to Winnipeg for the third game. That day, September 5, Arab terrorists hijacked the Olympic Games in Munich and killed 11 members of the Israeli team. Mahovlich interpreted the bloody incident as a Russian plot. On the bus ride to catch the Winnipeg plane, he spoke darkly of the Munich disaster to Arthur Harnett, the co-ordinator of the series telecast.

"That's the Russians for you," Mahovlich told Harnett.

"Oh, no, Frank," Harnett said. "The Arabs were responsible for those killings."

Mahov's attitude was ram rod rigid. "Don't tell me that the orders didn't come from head office in Moscow."

Big Frank was preoccupied with the Moscow menace in 1972, but for Team 74 to win on the morning of the first game, Mahovlich had to be well, and—most important —had to play well. There was no assurance of that, coming up to this first game. He was picked to play left wing with Ralph Backstrom and Howe, but the choice was apparently a toss-up between Mahovlich and Mark Howe. The younger Howes, Marty and Mark, were among the callow Canadians not dressed. Their father, in the paternal warmth that fathers sometimes express, had said that he'd consider it a rewarding experience to start an international hockey game in the same line-up as his sons.

That would have to wait. Harris wasn't thinking of a father-and-son story that would make pleasant reading 20 years down the road. He was going with his best, which the Howe kids in training camp had not been. Harris only hoped that his best wouldn't psych themselves out. He wanted them up, but not up-tight.

ROSTERS

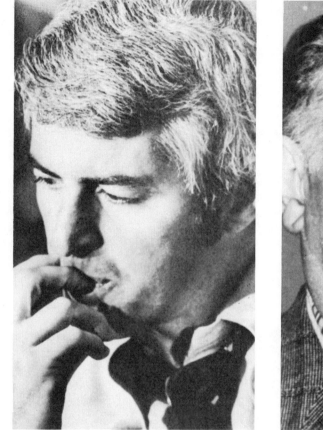

Coach Billy Harris of Team Canada.

Coach Boris Kulagin of the Soviet Selects.

TEAM CANADA

Goal: Gerry Cheevers, Don McLeod, Gilles Gratton.

Defence: J. C. Tremblay, Marty Howe, Paul Shmyr, Al Hamilton, Rick Smith, Rick Ley, Brad Selwood, Pat Stapleton.

Forwards: Ralph Backstrom, Jim Harrison, Mike Walton, Andre Lacroix, Serge Bernier, Pat Price, Frank Mahovlich, Paul Henderson, Bobby Hull, Mark Howe, Marc Tardiff, Gordie Howe, Rejean Houle, Tom Webster, Johnny MacKenzie, Bruce McGregor

USSR

Goal: Vladislav Tretiak, Alexander Sidelinkov, Vladimir Polupanov.

Defence: Alexander Gusev, Vladimir Lutchenko, Juri Liapkin, Valery Vasiljev, Gennadi Tsygankov, Victor Kuznetzov, Alexander Sapelkin, Alexander Filippov, Juri Fiodorov.

Forwards: Juri Lebedev, Alexander Maltsev, Boris Mikhailov, Alexander Bodunov, Alexander Yakushev, Vladimir Petrov, Viacheslav Anisin, Sergi Kapustin, Sergi Kotov, Valery Kharlamov, Vladimir Schadrin, Victor Shalimov, Konstanin Klimov, Vladimir Popov, Alexander Volchkov.

Bobby Hull scores Canada's second goal of the game in a
3-3 tie with the Soviets.

GAME ONE

CANADA 3—USSR 3

Line-ups

USSR
Goal: Tretiak, Sidelinkov.
Defence: Gusev, Lutchenko, Liapkin, Vasiljev, Tsygankov, Kuznetzov, Fiodorov.
Forwards: Lebedev, Maltsev, Mikhailov, Bodunov, Yakushev, Petrov, Anisin, Kapustin, Kotov, Kharlamov, Schadrin.

CANADA
Goal: Cheevers, McLeod.
Defence: Tremblay, Stapleton, Smith, Shmyr, Ley, Selwood.
Forwards: Hull, G. Howe, Mahovlich, Walton, Henderson, MacGregor, Lacroix, Houle, Bernier, Backstrom, McKenzie, Mark Howe.

First Period

1. Canada, McKenzie (Lacroix, Hull) 12:13

Penalties: None

Second Period

2. Russia, Luchenko (Tsygankov, Kapustin) 7:46
3. Canada, Hull (Walton, Howe) 12:07
4. Russia, Kharlamov (Vasiljev) 14:04
5. Russia, Petrov (Gusev, Kharlamov) 17:10

Penalties: Houle 0:24, McKenzie, Liapkin 4:24, Vasiljev 11:07, Selwood 12:40, Shmyr 14:38, 17:02

Third Period

6. Canada, Hull (Lacroix, McKenzie) 14:18
Penalties: Kasputin 6:04, Bodunov 15:16

Shots on goal

Russia	8	11	9—28
Canada	9	10	15—34

Gerry Cheevers, who played a strong game for Team
Canada, reaches for one of three that got by him.

September 17, Quebec City

—Team 74 was coming at the Soviet Nationals late in the third period, coming hard enough to untie a 3-3 tie, and Peter White turned to his *Globe and Mail* colleague in a tense, crowded press box.

"I guess," White observed, "this game takes the rocky out of the World Rocky Association."

Indeed. I had dismissed the World Hockey Association as the World Rocky Association on the basis of its artistic and financial flops.

But the night of September 17, gloomy and wet as autumn nights in Quebec City often are, was a night for several WHA mercenaries to get partly square to repeal cans of scorn thrown at them. They snapped at Soviet hands that would bleed them, unlucky not to win the first game of the Great International Ice Capade.

With 36 seconds left, Frank Mahovlich walked in on tall Vladislav Tretiak, close enough to see the bloodshot eyes of the Soviet goalkeeper. Mahovlich drove the puck wide.

The rubber ricocheted off the backboards and rebounded to Tretiak, who cuddled it and smothered the last Canadian chance. A goal there, by Mahovlich,

would have vindicated the Big M for an indifferent series two years ago.

Mahovlich toweled off in the Canadian quarters after the game, casual about it all and unsmiling, hardly the up-tight player that he had been portrayed.

"I was trying to put the puck up high," he explained to succeeding waves of elbowing reporters. "But Tretiak's body was twisted like a pretzel, with his body up. So I hammered the puck past the post. He made his move, I made mine, and he beat me."

Mahovlich held up his thumb and forefinger about a half inch apart.

"I shot maybe this wide."

Hockey is supposed to be a game for young legs, and Soviet youth would be served later in the series, but this one was for the beau ideals of the old folks set.

There was Gordon Howe, rising 47 and strolling a bit, but getting windshield wiper elbows up into the startled expression, particularly, of the precocious rookie, Sergei Kapustin. Young Kapustin woke up the next morning with a cauliflower chin.

"I thought this would be just another game," Howe said, cooling out, ruminating on it. "But you put on the Canadian sweater and realize that its

The Russians attack. Their passing was not as crisp as in the '72 series.

not just another game. Too many Canadians are counting on it."

The tooth of time had gnawed at him, and his hair is going away, but when Mahovlich blasted wide, Howe was waiting for the rebound.

"There were a couple of kids there," he mentioned, "just waiting to pounce."

Howe meant himself and Ralph Backstrom, who has not had many truant officers looking for him lately, either. Backstrom turned 37 and next day, on September 18.

"My greatest thrill," Howe said, "next to playing the first pro game with my boys, in Houston last winter."

Howe's kids, Mark and Marty, did not play in the first game, benched

because Team Canada's best may be their oldest.

"The pressure has been terrific on the boys," Howe said. "Mark got a migraine headache so bad two nights ago he couldn't sleep for worrying about the series. Marty's different. Before the game he got rubbed down and fell asleep on the trainers table."

Robert Marvin Hull had known worries before the game, his customary insouciance erased by tension. He was a super shooter, blackballed from Team 72 by a vindictive National Hockey League and the NHL Players Association. Hull had put everybody in the NHL in a dress shirt, from Clarence Campbell on down to R. Alan Eagleson, but they

barred him two years ago because he dared jump to the WHA.

"We'll take it," Hull said of the 3-3 tie, satisfied that his playmates were better than a tie. "We outskated them in the last ten minutes of the third period, which experts said couldn't happen. I think the Russians were sagging, not us."

Hull was asked to recreate his second goal, the one that deadlocked the Soviets 3-3. There were fewer than six minutes remaining when, allied with rambunctious John McKenzie, and under-rated Andre Lacroix, Hull unleashed a powerful wrist shot, in front, from 30 feet.

There was a high-beam grin on Hull, his choppers cheerfully bared. "I didn't

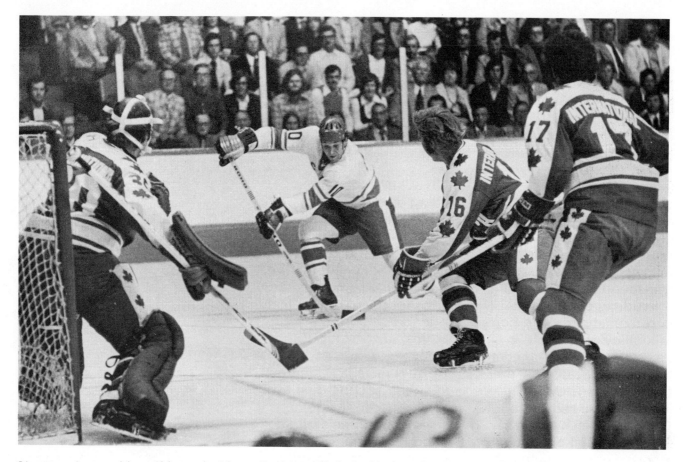

Cheevers braces himself for a shot from the face-off circle. He stopped 28 in tonight's game.

see it," he said of his snapping shot, "I just fired it."

A reporter for a morning newspaper, going for the downs against an impending deadline, demanded of Hull, "Okay, what did Team 74 do that Team 72 didn't, in the first game?"

Hull gazed at the harried press attaches, just the slightest edge on his benign disposition.

"Team 72 didn't know the facts just like some of you didn't. We knew the facts. We knew our forwards had to come back and help our defencemen. We knew we couldn't give 'em any 3-on-2 breaks, or 2-on-1, like Team 72 did."

There was some rah-rah in his assessment of his associates put down as raw-raw.

"Everybody in the room ought to know that Billy Harris can coach, and he doesn't need to yell. And that cancer put out about our defence was a bad rap. They proved the knockers wrong tonight."

Hull especially proved his detractors in the NHL wrong, the Establishment chaps who forever insist he is only out for himself. He was the key man in a team effort, the player who scored two Canadian goals, justifiably chosen the best in class.

A reporter suggested Hull should be glad to have it shoved down the NHL Establishment's throat, however momentarily.

"It was childish to blackball me in 1972," he said evenly. "But I don't hold much grudge. You have to forgive children."

There had been polite perfunctory claps for the Soviets when they were introduced, then a fulsome reception from 10,958 fans for the Canadians. There was a standing ovation for J. C. Tremblay, a crafty 37-year-old defenceman employed by the Quebec Nordiques. There was a standing response to Paul Henderson's white-helmeted appearance, lusty cheers for Hull, a 43-second ovation when Howe was announced.

`Then, while a red carpet was rolled out to centre ice, so Pierre Trudeau wouldn't

27

take a Prime Ministerial pratfall, the public address announcer spieled glorious glop about "this series mounting international fellowship . . . that transcends world barriers."

Trudeau dropped the ceremonial puck and Boris Mikhailov, the tough Soviet captain, beat the Canadian leader, Pat Stapleton, on the face off. They got Trudeau and red-haired Georgi Regulsky, a vice-president of the Soviet Sports Federation, out of there finally, and the game began only a trifling thirty-one minutes late.

Cowboy John McKenzie scored twelve minutes and thirteen seconds later, the first goal in another piece of hockey history, cruising in front to tip in Andre Lacroix's pass. The crowd erupted in gallic glee, singing a lively refrain that sounded, to English-listening ears, like "Youpi, youpi, youpi, youpi, yi!" Team 74 led 1-0 after twenty hectic minutes, but the Russians rebounded early in the second, the lofty Vladimir Loutchenko firing a screen shot, from the point, beyond the struggling reach of Gerry Cheevers. Hull restored the Canadian lead mid-way in the period on a power play. Howe dug the puck out from behind the Russian goal, shoveling

it to Mike Walton, then sitting on Gemmadi Tsygankov, the Soviet defenceman who tried to impede him. Walton slipped the puck back to the point to Hull, who lashed a baleful slapshot past Tretiak. That touched off another explosion of "Youpi, youpi, yi's!"

The Russians retaliated with their second goal two minutes later, the fleet Valery Kharlomov leaping through Tremblay and Stapleton at the Canadian defence, holding his balance, and tucking the puck up under the cross bar.

Before the period ended, a worthless cross-checking penalty by Paul Schmyr set up the third Russian goal. Vladimir Petrov, off to one side, punched Alexander Gusev's rebound into the net. The Russians remained ahead until 14:18 of the last period when, unable to hold off the freewheeling Canadians, they gave Hull room to shoot. That's been a mistake since Hull was a rookie, in 1958.

The noise was immense, the sort of cheering that inspired Jim Coleman to write in the Southam papers, "If Montcalm had been cheered so loudly against Wolfe that time in 1759, Canada would have been French forever."

Frank Mahovlich missed on this close-in shot in the dying moments of the game. A goal would have given the Canadians a win.

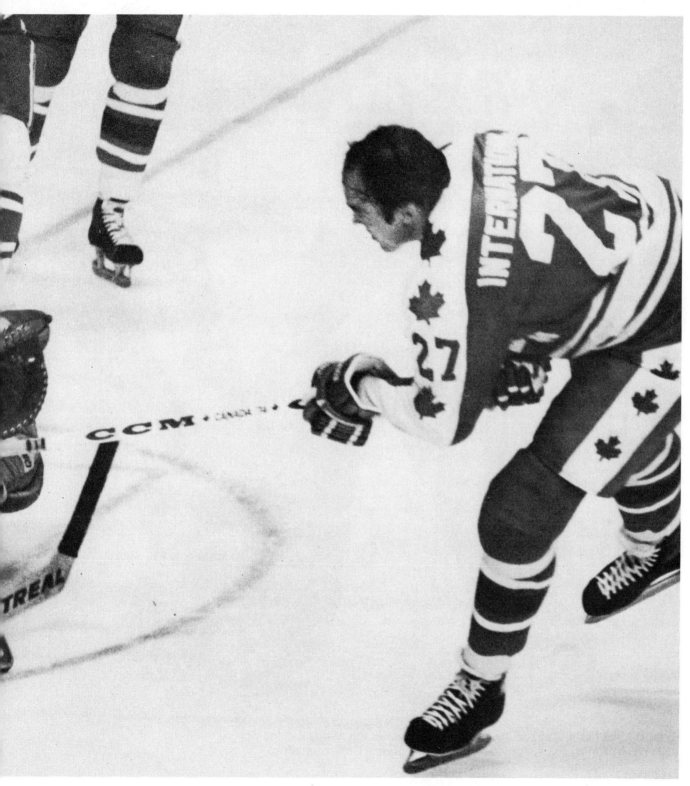

We did it. Canada scored their first win of the series 4-1 in Toronto. Here Paul Shmyr congratulates Cheevers after the game.

GAME TWO
CANADA 4—USSR 1

Line-ups

U.S.S.R.

Goal: Tretiak, Sidelinkov.

Defence: Gusev, Lutchenko, Liapkin, Vasiljev, Tsygankov, Kuznetzov, Fiodorov.

Forwards: Lebedev, Maltsev, Mikhailov, Bodunov, Yakushev, Petrov, Anisin, Kapustin, Kotov, Kharlamov, Schadrin.

CANADA

Goal: Cheevers, McLeod.

Defence: Tremblay, Stapleton, Smith, Shmyr, Ley, Selwood.

Forwards: Hull, Gordie Howe, Mahovlich, Walton, Henderson, MacGregor, Lacroix, Houle, Bernier, Backstrom, McKenzie, Mark Howe.

First Period

1. Canada, Backstrom (Mark Howe, G. Howe) 4:31.
2. Canada, Lacroix (McKenzie, Tremblay) 10:49.

Penalties: Smith 1:44; Kapustin 10:19; Kapustin 12:50; Mahovlich 16:08.

Second Period

3. Canada, Hull (Lacroix, McKenzie) 2:50.
4. Russia, Yakushev (Schadrin, Lebedev) 13:09.

Penalties: Mahovlich 9:44; Lacroix 15:39.

Third Period

5. Canada, Tremblay (Lacroix, Hull) 17:03.

Penalties: Smith 13:23; Maltsev 16:04; Tremblay 19:00.

Shots on Goal

Russia	13	8	9—30
Canada	10	16	7—33

Vladislav Tretiak reaches in vain for Andre Lacroix's shot
which put Canada ahead 2-0 in the first period.

September 19, Toronto

—Hockey is the Canadian specific, as poet Al Purdy put it, never more so than when there is a challenge to our supremacy in the one game that grabs this country by the short ends of the soul.

Thus tonight in Maple Leaf Gardens, the old Tajmahockey on Carlton Street, when Team Canada 74 was introduced opposite Squad Soviet in the second game of their second Super Bowlski:

The Canadians stood at their blue line, skates shifting a little, each one stepping forward when his name was announced to receive the accolades of the 16,485 fans in attendance. The best was saved for last.

"And No. 27," bleated the announcer, "Frank Mahovlich."

The crowd roared its approval, a sound big Frank was unaccustomed to during his tenure with Punch Imlach and his serfs.

Next: "No. 16 . . . Bobby Hull." The Golden Jet of the Winnipeg Jets, new rug and all, smiled for the fans who rose to greet him. WHA or not, Hull was still the Golden Boy of the NHL. The applause must have been, in part, for his part in establishing the World Hockey Association. Without him, doubtless, there would be less of a WHA than there is now.

Gordie was introduced last, and for 43 seconds the waves of applause echoed through the rafters of Harold Ballard's cashbox on Carlton Street. The crowd loved him.

In the press box, Wren Blair offered a comment.

"You know what those ovations mean? For Mahovlich and Hull and Howe? It means more than the World Hockey Association against National Hockey League. Its a hockey people simply saying thanks for what these three have given to a hockey country."

And Billy Harris had come home to the Gardens, where he had played some of the best hockey of his career.

"This has to be the biggest game ever for me here. This is my home town, this is one great team I'm coaching and we're playing against an equally talented team. I feel more pressure tonight than at any other point since we selected the team."

Team Canada was not blown out of the rink into the St. Lawrence River as many had expected them to be in the first game of the series two nights previously in Quebec City. They tied the Soviet side 3-3 and should have won it. Tonight, they were playing in the friendly confines of Maple Leaf Gardens, a cozy old place that welcomed Team WHA as they would welcome their own Maple Leafs. Harris was standing behind the bench his Toros would be using in the coming season. With the exception of a fireplace, an

old dog and a pair of slippers, things couldn't have been more correct or comfortable. The Good Guys were going to win tonight; even the referee was going to help.

The success of the Quebec City draw was evident as play started. The game was fast and chippy from the opening face-off. Rick Smith, a former

defenceman for the Boston Bruins who has seen more than a little ice time at these same Gardens, received a penalty at 1:44 of the first period for elbowing, a trick he must have learned from Howe, the Old Master himself. Canada killed the penalty, helped by the lack of crisp passing on the the Soviets' part that has been so evident in their

Lacroix, Hull and Tremblay, Bill Harris had a look of concern on his face after the game. He didn't think that his team played as well tonight as they had in Quebec City despite their decisive win, but "I thought it was a gutsy performance."

Hull was still hurting from the exhibition series knee injury, and now Howe had an ailment. Paul Henderson and Frank Mahovlich had shown little to date, and Harris must have been painfully aware of this fact. Andre Lacroix and Paul Shmyr had outstanding games, as did Gerry Cheevers, who made two sensational stops in the last ten minutes to keep the Soviets out of the game.

The old Bugaboo— refereeing—popped up again tonight in the form of good old Tom Brown, a man who is a kickback to the fairness and honesty of *Tom Brown's Schooldays* fame. With about two minutes gone in the third period, Russian forward Vladimir Petrov fired a blazing wrist shot past Cheevers that hit the crossbar and went into the net, then popped out. Everyone in the country saw the goal except Brown. Canada was leading 3-1 at the time, and as it turned out the final result wouldn't have been any different had Brown allowed the goal.

previous games. Ralph Backstrom shot the Canadian side into the lead at 4:31 when he converted snappy passes from Mark and Gordie Howe into the Russian goal.

In his next shift following the goal, Gordie was taken off with what proved to be bruised ribs, and by the end of the first period was in his street clothes.

"I have no idea what happened," Gordie said. "Perhaps I strained them congratulating Mark on the fine pass he made."

"I had X-rays taken and there's nothing broken, so I guess I'll be all right to play in Winnipeg if the coach wants me."

The coach wanted him. Even though Team Canada went on to win 4-1 behind

"It was a disgrace that Brown took a goal away from the Russians," said that renowned advocate of fair play, Harold Ballard. "The puck was in the net and should have counted. I want Canada to win, but I want 'em to win fairly."

The goal light was on, and stayed on for some time. But Brown overruled the goal judge. Brown said that neither he nor his linesmen saw the puck go in, and the goal judge hesitated.

"I'm not going to count a goal when a goal judge hesitates," Brown said.

The Russians weren't about to pack their bags and go home, but they were upset about the call.

Kulagin said that it was "... an undisputable goal and no doubt upset us .... I hope I don't see that referee again."

The Soviets were professional enough to realize that they wouldn't have won the game anyhow if the call had gone in their favour. But from that point on they were frustrated, and it showed in their play. They came close, but didn't score again, and Tremblay put the game on ice when he scored Canada's final goal at 17:03 of the third.

Team Canada is ahead 1-0-1, and now on to Winnipeg, home of Hull. It would be next to impossible to lose there. Victor Dombrowski of Russia is to be the referee, Team Canada is to win, and the country is to be convinced that the first two games haven't been flukes. Watch out, Russians. The Jet is coming home.

(Top) GOAL! Bobby Hull pops one to make it 3-0 Canada.

(Bottom) Cheevers makes a big save off Valery Kharlamov to preserve the Canadian lead.

(Right) This picture of the disputed goal seems to indicate that the puck was in.

36

Alexander Yakushev fires the puck past Don McLeod in the first period to tie the game up 1-1 for the Soviets.

GAME THREE

USSR 8—CANADA 5

Line-ups

U.S.S.R.

Goal: Tretiak, Sidelinkov.

Defence: Gusev, Lutchenko, Liapkin, Vasiljev, Tsygankov, Kuznetsov, Filippov.

Forwards: Volchkov, Maltsev, Lebedev, Mikhailov, Yakushev, Petrov, Kharlamov, Schadrin, Anisin, Bodunov, Shalimov.

CANADA

Goal: McLeod, Gratton.

Defence: Tremblay, Marty Howe, Stapleton, Smith, Shmyr, Hamilton.

Forwards: Walton, Lacroix, Webster, Mark Howe, Backstrom, Harrison, Hull, Henderson, MacGregor, Bernier, Tardif McKenzie.

First Period

1. Canada, MacGregor (Henderson) 14:58.
2. Russia, Yakushev (Schadrin) 17:25.

Penalties: Lacroix 5:02; Smith 13:25; Walton 19:16.

Second Period

3. Russia, Mikhailov (Petrov) 1:23.
4. Canada, Webster (Bernier, Tardif) 12:40.
5. Russia, Vasiljev (Mikhailov, Petrov) 15:14.
6. Russia, Maltsev (Anisin) 15:31.

Penalties: Hamilton 3:26; McKenzie 5:49; Kuznetsov 5:49; Schadrin 8:16; McKenzie 13:24; Lebedev 13:24.

Third Period

7. Russia, Yakushev (Schadrin) 2:35.
8. Russia, Bodunov 8:44.
9. Russia, Yakushev 11:27.
10. Canada, Henderson (Harrison) 14:31.
11. Canada, Henderson (Harrison, MacGregor) 15:04.
12. Canada, Bernier (Webster, Hamilton) 16:01.
13. Russia, Lebedev (Lutchenko) 18:05.

Penalties: Kuznetsov 12:20; Lutchenko 18:56.

Shots on Goal

Russia	11	16	12—39
Canada	8	14	12—34

All eyes are on the puck as McLeod braces himself for the shot. Tremblay and Harrison defend for Team Canada.

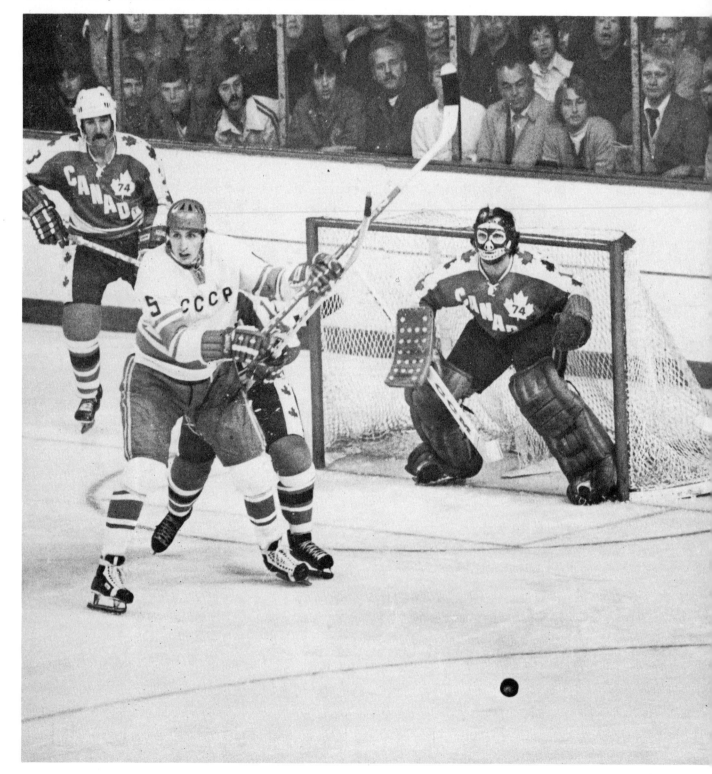

September 21, Winnipeg

—Bill Harris took a calculated gamble tonight and lost. After skating with the Soviets in the first two games of the series, the Canadians were defeated 8-5 to tie the series at a win, a loss, and a tie apiece.

"We gambled and we lost," assessed Harris after the game. "If we had beaten them today, we would have won the series today."

That's a fair comment by the Team Canada coach. If they had gone to Vancouver two games up it would have been difficult for the Soviets to come back, even with the second half of the series being played in Moscow.

"But the worst that could happen," continued Harris in a philosophical vein, "was that the series would be tied. We weren't embarassed and I'd make the same decision again, considering the circumstances."

The circumstances were that the coach had promised all of his players that they'd get into the series, an attempt to avoid the defections suffered by Team Canada 72 in Moscow. And Harris picked Winnipeg to make the changes. If the lesser pros had played and won, all would be well. If they lost,

which they did, the series would be tied and Canada would go on to Vancouver with a tie, with one home game left to take the series lead. And Harris would be sure that the substitutes remained precisely that.

Don McLeod of Houston, the Howes' teammate, was in goal for Gerry Cheevers, but in Harris' estimation, "the way the Soviets played today, they probably would have scored seven-eight goals on Gerry."

That's a difficult statement to back up, especially since Cheevers has played superbly in the first two games. There's no reason to expect that things would have changed in Winnipeg. Jim Harrison, Marty Howe, Al Hamilton and Tom Webster replaced Frank Mahovlich, Gordie Howe, Rejean Houle, Rick Ley and Brad Selwood for this game as well. Harris said that his reason for the changes was fatigue. His players were tired.

"Even Bobby Hull was drifting and getting caught out of position. I knew that three games in five days would begin to show. Now, some players are rested for the important fourth game in Vancouver."

The fourth game would have taken on less importance had the

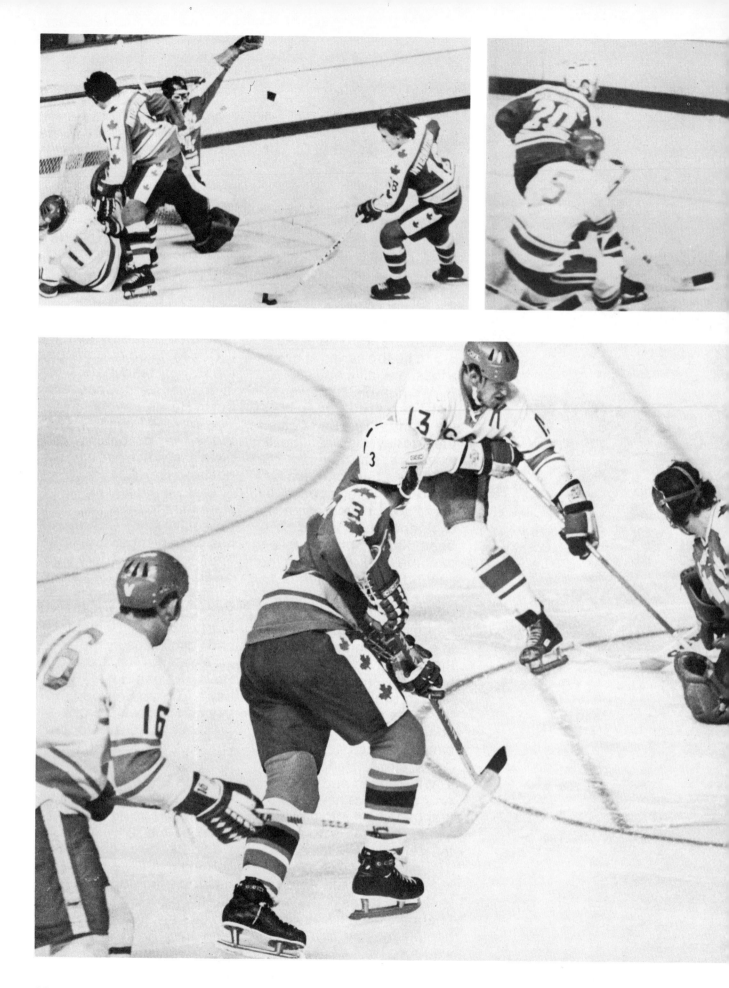

(Left) One of many close calls! Shmyr and Smith cover up as Lebedev slides into the Canadian net dring early action.

(Right) Bruce MacGregor shoots high into the net to open the scoring. Covering up is Juri Liapkin.

(Lower) The Russians score one of eight against McLeod. Tremblay can't get there soon enough to be of much help.

Canadians won tonight, but Harris' move is not unjustified. Over the first two games Gordie Howe had two assists, but he was hurting this afternoon from the rib injury picked up in Game 2. Mahovlich, Ley, Houle and Selwood had been held off the scoresheet. In the game a goal and an assist, Harrison two assists, and Hamilton an assist. So, based on offensive past performance, the move was a good one.

Defensively it was a different story. Of the substitutes, only Webster made a good account of himself. McLeod let the puck slip by him eight times, something that likely would not have happened had Cheevers been tending goal. Hamilton looked as if he was in slow motion. Marty gave up the puck once that led to a Russian goal. But he probably hit the nail squarely when he said that the absence of his father gave the Russians a decided edge.

"The Russians worship him."

Victor Dombrowski of the Soviet Union handled the game, and as usual the officiating left much to be desired.

"I couldn't believe that referee," said Marty Howe, whose play at times couldn't be believed either. "I lost my stick and I must have punched a Russian five times in front of the net. The ref raised his arm and I thought I was gone for sure. Then, he dropped it, and there was no penalty."

Dombrowski made assorted calls during the game, most of them brutal. One of the strangest was a penalty shot awarded to the Russian team. He apparently felt that the sooner he awarded a penalty shot to the Russians to make up for the one given the Canadians in Toronto, the better. Maltsev took the shot and drove it high.

Boris Kulagin was so incensed about the work of Tom Brown in Toronto that he'll refuse to use him in any further games. Harris said the same about Dombrowski.

Bodies are all over the ice as McLeod comes out to cover
up. Moving in are Shmyr, Smith and Hull.

Personnel changes and officiating aside, the Russians deserve full credit for their play.

"I think they just pulled themselves together," said smiling Boris. "We played much better hockey, but then it does seem that Canada played worse. In Quebec, they played stronger, but we were weaker."

True. The Canadians looked inept at times. They came up flat after their win in Toronto. The first period ended in a 1-1 tie, with Russia outshooting Canada 11-8, and Canada took the only penalties of the period.

The Russians turned it on in the second, scoring four times to the Canadians' once. Play became chippy, with McKenzie picking up two roughing penalties and taking Russian players to the box with him both times. But the Russians were beating the Canadians at their hitting game, and giving just as good as they received.

It was all over before the third period started, but the third, with the exception of Paul Henderson's two goals within 33 seconds and Bernier's goal less than a minute later to narrow the count to 7-5, was all Russia. Lebedev put it away with the final Russian goal less than two minutes away from the final bell.

It was a rather poor show on Team Canada's part, both on the ice and after the game. Had it not been for the three goal flurry in the third, the score woud have been 7-2 for Russia. There were no bad penalty calls against the Canadians to account for their lack of attack in the third; they were simply outplayed. But excuse was piled onto excuse for the Canadian loss.

Harris made the line-up changes; that lost it for us. The Russians had a psychological edge; that lost it for us. Team Canada was not accustomed to playing in the afternoon; that made the difference. The two quick Russian goals (by Vasiljev and Maltsev) in the second period made the difference, because we lost our confidence. The Russians stationed a man in front of the net, which we weren't used to. Canadians are used to playing 78 games to warm up for a series like this, such as the Stanley Cup or Avco Cup series. The Russians aren't. That made a difference.

It all boils down to one thing—we lost. Despite all the excuses, Billy Harris summed it up quite adequately in the end.

"Just to have those big guys out of there made it easier for the Russians, but it comes down to the fact that we simply let the Russians play the game their way."

Indeed.

Gordie Howe scores one in the first period. Ralph Backstrom, whose play has been brilliant in the series,
assisted.

GAME FOUR
CANADA 5—USSR 5

Line-ups

U.S.S.R.
Goal: Tretiak, Sidelinkov.
Defence: Gusev, Lutchenko, Liapkin, Vasiljev, Tsygankov, Kuznetsov, Sapelkin.
Forwards: Maltsev, Lebedev, Mikhailov, Yakushev, Petrov, Kharlamov, Schadrin, Anisin, Bodunov, Klimov, Volchkov.

CANADA
Goal: Cheevers, McLeod.
Defence: Stapleton, Ley, Tremblay, Shmyr, Smith, Marty Howe.
Forwards: Walton, Houle, Lacroix, Gordie Howe, Mark Howe, Backstrom, Hull, Henderson, MacGregor, Bernier, McKenzie, Mahovlich.

First Period

1. Russia, Vasiljev (Kharlamov) 3:34.
2. Canada, G. Howe (Stapleton, Backstrom) 4:20.
3. Russia, Mikhailov (Petrov) 5:59.
4. Canada, Hull (Mahovlich) 12:45.
5. Canada, Hull (Stapleton) 15:11.
6. Canada, Mahovlich (Bernier, Houle) 17:10.
7. Canada, Hull (Lacroix) 17:45.

Penalty: Gusev 11:38.

Second Period

8. Russia, Yakushev (Lebedev) 11:04.

Penalties: Shmyr 4:08; Petrov 13:35; Smith 13:35; Ley 17:07.

Third Period

9. Russia, Maltsev 16:08.
10. Russia, Gusev (Mikhailov, Petrov) 16:59.

Penalties: Schadrin 6:45; McKenzie 7:30; McKenzie 10:26; Tsygankov 17:51.

Shots on Goal

Russia	12	10	6—28
Canada	11	8	9—28

Frank Mahovlich, who has been continually thwarted at the Russian goal, scores his first of the series in the first period.

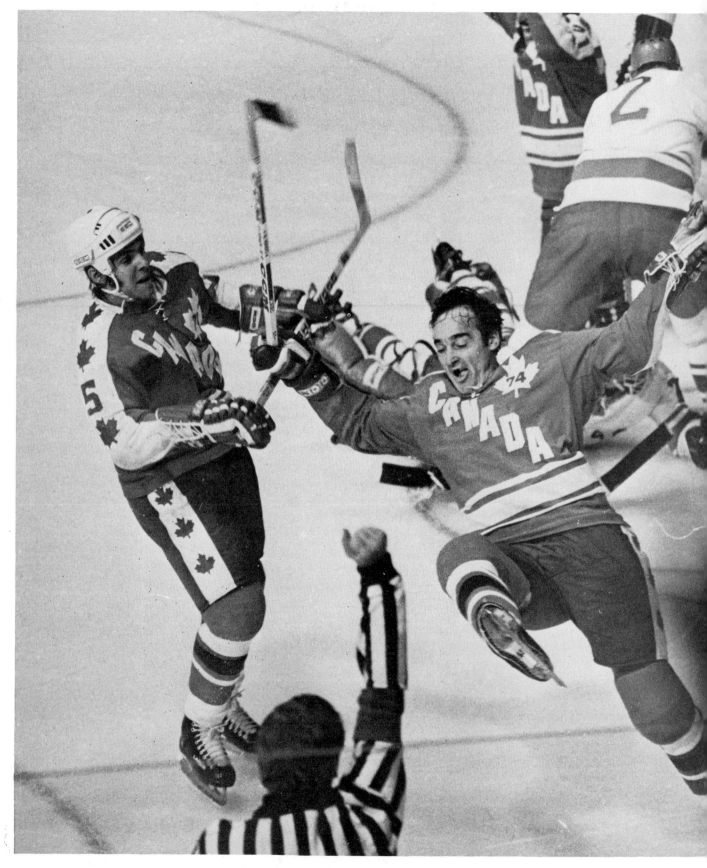

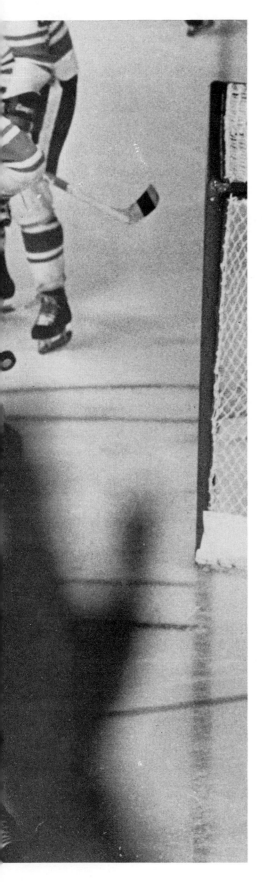

September 23, Vancouver

—We blew it. Canada skated into the dressing room tonight after 20 minutes with a 5-2 lead that should have been enough to put the game away right there. But they forgot to skate for the rest of the game, and the Soviets outscored Canada 3-0 over the final 40 minutes to salvage a 5-5 tie. Team Canada now heads for Moscow with the series all tied up. They should be ahead 3 games to 1 or, if you insist on faulting Harris for the 8-5 debacle two nights ago, 4-0. But the score board doesn't usually lie.

Bobby Hull blasted three bombs behind Tretiak in the Russian nets in the first, likely among three of the finest he's ever scored.

"It felt marvelous when those three went in, but I can't look back on this game with any satisfaction whatever because we blew it.

"We had them down and we couldn't hold them there.

"Perhaps we can learn from our mistakes. Maybe we'll all realize that anything less than a total 60-minute effort is not enough against these fellows."

There seemed to be something missing in this game for the Canadians. Maybe it was just the fact that they were playing in Vancouver. Here in 1972 Team Canada was hooted unmercifully on its way to a 5-2 loss. Who could forget it? And Phil Esposito's impassioned plea after the game, appealing to the country's patriotism, appealing to the fact that Team Canada 72 had given a lot up for the series, including money and their vacations, to play for their country. It possibly made a difference in '74.

Other unsettling things came to the surface in this game which inspire misgivings for the Moscow half, besides blowing the big lead.

The Russians were obviously improving, possibly overcoming the travel weariness of the first two games.

The Canadians again weren't sharp and alert in the second and third periods, similar to the situation in Winnipeg.

With the exception of Marty Howe in the line-up, paired with J. C. Tremblay, the team was the same one that soundly trounced the Soviets in Toronto. With the exception of the first period, they fell far below their second game performance.

With the exception of a first period goal tonight, Frank Mahovlich was distant, and he has contributed very little thus far. As in 1972, possibly the thought of travelling to Moscow was on his mind.

Mike Walton's play was erratic.

There were still a lot of senseless penalties. In Game 1 it had been Paul

Shmyr who took the senseless trips to the penalty box. Since then, Johnny McKenzie has been the culprit. His two minor penalties three minutes apart in the third period of tonight's game prevented the Canadian offence from organizing and popping the winner, something they might have done with the extra four minutes of play. As the headline on the sports page of the *Toronto Sun* claimed, McKenzie's sins really hurt us.

Harris didn't seem overly bothered by McKenzie's misdemeanours.

"He picked up a few penalties tonight, but he's been a real spark plug in all four games. When a player gets tired its hard to change his habits and Johnny McKenzie played tonight the only way he knows how —all out."

Let's change the subject. Johnny may have been the bad guy, but the team didn't exactly melt the ice after the first period. They thought they had it won, and went into a defensive shell. The Russians sensed this, and went after them.

The officiating received the usual withering blast of criticism, depending on who you were listening to. The Soviets collected four penalties, Team Canada five, but Waldo Szczapek, the Polish referee, turned a blind eye to many infractions.

The first three goals in the game were scored within two minutes and twenty-five seconds of each other in the

first period. The Canadians had difficulty in clearing the puck in the early minutes, and persistence paid off for the Russians when Vasiliev scored on a pass from Kharlomov at 3:34. Howe got that one back from Stapleton and Backstrom less than a minute later, but Mikhailov put the Russians

ahead at 5:59. Then Hull went to work.

"We've heard of Bobby Hull before as a player of outstanding ability and outstanding moral features," Kulagin said after the game, "and we have now witnessed them for ourselves. He is a man of exceptional ability, and a

(Opposite) Three of the series' big guns are shown here in the third period—for Canada, Hull and Mahovlich; for Russia, Mikhailov.

(Left) Action around the Russian goal. Tremblay and Bernier watch Mahovlich fire the puck past Tretiak.

(Lower) Stapleton changes direction to chase a Russian near-miss in the second period. Russia scored two in the third for the tie.

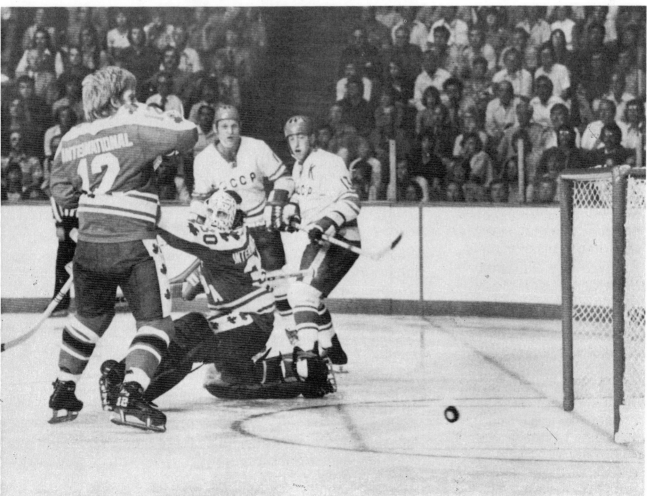

real gentleman. Time does not seem to tell on him."

And a superb performance it was. After a slashing penalty to Gusev, Mahovlich sent a pass to Hull, who blasted a low slap shot from the point that completely fooled Tretiak. That tied up the game. At 15:11 Stapleton passed off to Hull, and sent the Jet in alone. After a goal by Mahovlich, Hull got his third of the period on a wrist shot to Tretiak's stick side.

After that, it was all Russia. It may have been the stifling heat of the arena, or the fact that Team Canada just let up. In any case, the Russians came back with three goals before the end of the game to tie it up. They were beaten after the first, but wouldn't give up.

Thus the Canadian half of the series came to an end. The Canadians are to leave tomorrow for Helsinki for a game against the Finns, then on to Sweden for an exhibition match against the Swedish national team. They leave Canada one tie up on the '72 Canadian team, and with high hopes that they can at least gain a saw-off on Russian ice.

How they will manage on the wider ice surface in Moscow is a matter of conjecture. The old legs will have another 15 feet of ice surface width to negotiate, and from the way things looked in Winnipeg and the last two periods in Vancouver, this could present a problem.

The Russians will be a lot tougher on home ice. In every game thus far

(Left) Heavy action in front of the Russian goal.

(Lower) Gusev ties it up for Russia late in the third.

(Right) Howe demonstrates how to effectively keep your man down.

they have improved over their performance in Quebec City, and were obviously gearing for Moscow. They'll be tough. But it can be said that no matter what happens in Moscow, Canada must have a great deal of admiration for Team 74. They did much better than most sceptics expected, and they can leave Canada with their heads high. They have played good hockey against a younger Russian team.

"I think we're all right," Pat Stapleton said. "We now have valuable time to look everything over and that's got to help . . . . We all feel like we've accomplished quite a lot, since nobody expected us to do this well."

Nobody really expected there'd be a series left after the Vancouver game was over. There is, but the series is only half over.

Cheevers makes another big save from a Soviet player almost in the clear.

GAME FIVE

USSR 3—CANADA 2

Line-ups

RUSSIA

Goal: Tretiak, Sidelinkov.

Defence: Gusev, Lutchenko, Vasiljev, Tsygankov, Kuznetsov, Shatalov, Tiurin.

Forwards: Maltsev, Lebedev, Mikhailov, Petrov, Kharlamov, Vikulov, Schadrin, Anisin, Bodunov, Kotov, Shalimov.

CANADA

Goal: Cheevers, McLeod.

Defence: Ley, Tremblay, Selwood, Stapleton, Smith, Shmyr.

Forwards: Walton, Houle, Lacroix, Webster, G. Howe, Mark Howe, Backstrom, Hull, Henderson, Bernier, McKenzie, Mahovlich.

First Period

1. Russia, Maltsev (Vikulov, Anisin) 5:34.

Penalties: Mahovlich 2:32; Petrov 6:59; Ley 18:52; Bernier 15:07.

Second Period

2. Canada, G. Howe (Backstrom, Marty Howe) 00:15.
3. Russia, Maltsev (Schadrin, Vikulov) 15:04.

Penalties: Webster 4:14; Lebedev 7:02; McKenzie 13:52; Kharlamov 18:52; Bernier 18:52.

Third Period

4. Russia, Gusev 11:48.
5. Canada, Mark Howe (Shmyr) 18:10.

Penalties: Lacroix 2:46; Backstrom 4:37; Schadrin 5:38; Bodunov 16:21.

Shots on goal

Canada	8	4	4—16
Russia	9	10	8—27

Rick Ley takes a poke at Vladimir Petrov in the second period. Both went off for five minutes.

October 1, Moscow

—Team Canada was defeated 3-2 by the Soviets tonight. It was inevitable. Everything had gone wrong from the time the Canadians stepped off the plane from Sweden the night before until they stepped on the ice at Luzhniki Arena. And even then it didn't end.

The flight was late, and the players were caught up in the red tape of customs and immigration. The lobby at Moscow International airport was jammed. It took the team 2½ hours to check into their quarters at the Rossiya Hotel; but during that time, they had missed the practice time reserved for them at the arena.

"I'm sorry to miss the practice the day before a game, especially in the rink where we'll be playing," said Billy Harris after the fact. "It's a strange ice surface and a completely strange atmosphere.

"We'll have to hope they can get the feel of the place and of the ice surface in our morning session."

Bruce MacGregor had the flu.

The hotel was crowded, accommodations were poor.

And Gerry Cheevers' father-in-law died back in Toronto after collapsing at the Gardens during the second game.

A depressing start.

2200 fans were on hand to greet the Canadian team, but, unlike the '72 series, they were far below their noisy standard during Game 5. They were constantly outshouted by their Soviet counterparts, another signal, perhaps, of inevitable defeat.

It was a game Ivan the Terrible would have enjoyed, perhaps even invented during one of his bloodier interludes.

"We were lucky we didn't start the Third World War," Gordie Howe observed after it was all over.
then it didn't end.

The flight was late, and the players were caught up in the red tape of customs and immigration. The lobby at Moscow International airport was packed. All in all, it took the team 2½ hours to check into their quarters at the Rossiya Hotel; but during that time, they had missed the practice time reserved for them at the arena.

The so-called Friendly Series (remember all the speech-making in Quebec City) degenerated quickly into a pig sticking match early in the first period, with Soviet Borris Mikhailov taking a few chops at Cheevers' feet on the way by. From that point onward

(Left) A strong Russian defence, as shown here, helped the Soviets skate off with a 3-2 victory.

(Below) Tretiak dives out to take the puck from Mike Walton's stick and preserve the Russian triumph.

it was all downhill. Polish referee Waldo Szczypak handled this one, and he was the only one in the rink who seemed oblivious to what was going on. The Russians played perhaps their most aggressive game, and the Canadians retaliated blow for blow.

"Oh, the Russians trip and hook, all right," Gordie continued. "They slash you pretty good. But we're not angels, are we?"

Not exactly. But there was even some time to do a bit of scoring between he spears and slashes.

The first Russian goal came early in the first period. Maltsev scored his third of the series after a quick pass from Vikulov. Henderson and Selwood helped with this one by missing on clearing attempts in their own zone.

Frank Mahovlich had taken a minor earlier, but at 6:59 of the first period Ley and Petrov engaged in a shoving match, the rewards of which sent them both off. The period ended 1-0 for the Soviets, but not before the Canadians had made some determined efforts to destroy some of the Russians. Marty Howe seemed to have it in for Valery Kharlamov, and repeatedly ran at him, keeping it up during the night. Not that Kharlomov didn't deserve it; Howe just made it too obvious.

The Great One scored only fifteen seconds into the second of a pass from Ralph Backstrom that Gordie grabbed behind the net and tucked into the right side of the crease behind Tretiak. It was a good goal, and confirmed Howe as the most consistent Canadian performer on the ice tonight.

The second Russian goal, and Maltsev's second of the game, came at 15:04. Johnny McKenzie was the bad boy on this one again, as he seemed to be at least twice in Canada. McKenzie was resting in the penalty box after a cheap hooking penalty when the Russian scored.

Gusev put the game out of reach with nine minutes remaining in the third period, after picking up Kharlamov's rebound of a wide shot and firing it behind Cheevers, who was off balance. Mark Howe scored with less than two minutes remaining by holding onto the puck and shooting himself while the Soviets left him unguarded and concentrated on other Canadian shooters whom they felt should be scoring. Team Canada attempted to pull Cheevers for an extra attacker, but the Russians played excellent puck control hockey to prevent the Canadians from taking control. In fact, Cheevers made one of his best saves of the night in the final minute.

The 3-2 score was flattering to the Canadian side. Without Cheevers, who was selected as the best Canadian on the ice after the game, the score could easily have been 5 or 6 for the Russians. Cheevers was particularly brilliant in the first and second periods, when he repeated dazzling stops during Russian power plays that kept the Canadians at least superficially in the game.

After the match, Harris was typically low key, describing the refereeing as "inconsistent, . . . but adequate by international standards."

Realistically, the officiating was anything but adequate. As if to indicate that he really didn't mean what he already said, the coach left the media with a thought.

"Amateur refereeing can lead to chippiness because of its inconsistency."

It was more than chippiness. It was war. Both Gordie Howe and Ralph Backstrom objected strenuously to the refereeing. For his efforts, Backstrom earned a 10-minute misconduct in the third period which didn't help Our Side at all.

"Kharlamov and I were going for the puck near the boards," Ralph recounted later. "He kicked my feet from under me, right in front of the referee, but that lovely chap didn't see the trip. I had some warm things to say to the referee."

Gordie Howe filled in the sordid details.

"Backstrom really called the referee a stupid, expletive-deleted Polish homer. I'd have been disturbed if I'd been called a homer, too. That's real badmouthing."

The officiating must have been ludicrous for Backstrom to protest loudly enough to draw a misconduct. He hasn't had one in 12 years.

The entire team was frustrated with the officiating and it showed. Even with Harris' insistence on gentlemanly conduct, he couldn't hold his players down tonight. The match consistently threatened to turn into a brawl. It was an international Polish joke.

It's reasonable to say that the Canadians would have lost no matter who was officiating and it rankled. Mahovlich observed, "many things were done with spectacular inefficiency...."

"I think we've reached a point where we need to get more mileage out of our big men," said Hull, somewhat disappointed because he didn't get more ice time. "I think we're physically ready to cut back to three lines and give a few people more ice time."

In spite of Team Canada's weakest game to date, Hull and Howe still feel that they can beat the Soviets.

"Yeah, we'll win if we continue to get the type of goaltending we've been getting," said Bobby.

In addition, he should have said, some of the others are going to have to get off their behinds and get to work. Henderson and Walton in particular have been particularly inconspicuous. You can't win without scoring goals.

Paul Shmyr picks up the rebound after a close call at the Canadian end.

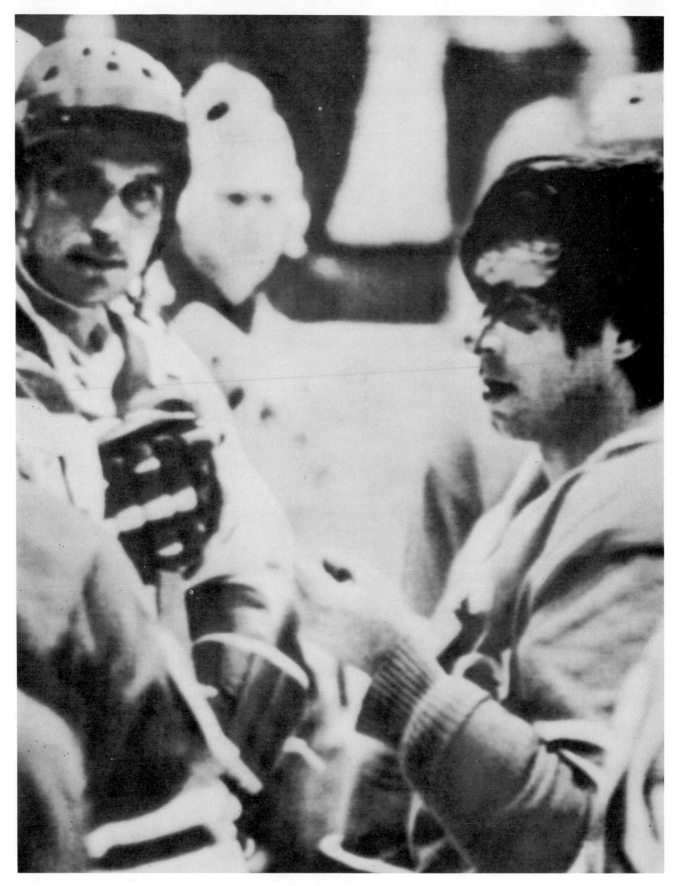

War! Kharlamov's face is bloodied after a post-game fight
with Rick Ley, who retaliated against Soviet tactics in Canada's 5-2 loss.

GAME SIX

USSR 5—CANADA 2

Line-ups
RUSSIA
Goal: Tretiak, Sidelinkov.
Defence: Gusev, Lutchenko, Vasiljev, Kuznetsov, Shatalov,
    Tiurin, Tsygankov.
Forwards: Maltsev, Lebedev, Mikhailov, Petrov, Kharlamov,
    Vikulov, Schadrin, Anisin, Bodunov, Kapustin, Yakushev.

CANADA
Goal: Cheevers, McLeod.
Defence: Stapleton, Ley, Tremblay, Marty Howe, Smith, Shmyr.
Forwards: McKenzie, Lacroix, Hull, G. Howe, Mark Howe, Houle,
    Bernier, Tardif, Henderson, Mahovlich, MacGregor,
    Backstrom.

First Period

1. Russia, Mikhailov (Kharlamov) 0:34.
2. Russia, Vasiljev (Kharlamov) 2:43.
3. Canada, Houle (Shmyr) 15:56.

Penalties: Mark Howe 0:53; Smith 16:38; Tardif 16:38.

Second Period

4. Canada, G. Howe (Mark Howe) 6:15.
5. Russia, Anisin (Vikulov) 8:22.
6. Russia, Shatalov (Tsygankov) 13:57.

Penalties: Mark Howe 12:22; MacGregor 12:44; Vasiljev 12:44.

Third Period

7. Russia, Kharlamov (Vikulov) 13:00.

Penalties: Smith 10:54; Kharlamov 1:54; Lebedev 15:04; Marty
    Howe 15:04; Ley 20:00.

Shots on goal

Canada	13	9	6—28
Russia	14	8	7—29

This headless Canadian chases the puck behind the net as the goal judge looks on with some foreboding.

October 3, Moscow

—In Canada, the NHL was suspending Steve Durbano of the Pittsburgh Penguins for swinging his stick at a goalie, the City of Toronto was threatening groups that use city ice to stop fights or lose their ice time, and in Russia team coach Boris Kulagin was calling for the jailing of Rickey Ley for attacking Valery Kharlamov after the game was over. The game was the Great International Bloodbath.

Team Canada 74: neither winners nor gentlemen, screamed a totally unsympathetic press corps.

All the high hopes of Canada drowned in a 5-2 loss tonight that bars the country from anything but a tie should they win the final two games of the series. All the fine diplomatic intentions were obliterated by the image of one bloody face.

Ley gave Kharlamov a thorough post-game pummelling that left the Russian's face bloodied and the crowd—Canadians included—shocked and disgusted. Kharlamov emerged from a player pile-up, which included a slight skirmish between Paul Shmyr and Boris Mikhailov, with blood streaming from his forehead and eye area. To his credit, he skated off the ice without emotion, showing no sign of pain.

Harris didn't retreat under the critical onslaught after the game. He backed up his boys. Harris tried to take the heat off by pouncing on a second period fight involving Bruce MacGregor and Valery Vasiljev. The incident brought five-minute fighting penalties for both.

"According to my international rule book the player who starts a fight—who first swings at an opponent—should get a 10-minute penalty. Vasiljev had already received a minor penalty when the fight started," Harris said. "He should have been given a total of 12 minutes."

Soviet referee Victor Dombrowski lost control.

In the prelude to the main event, Ley checked Kharlamov into the boards in the Canadian zone. Kharlamov retaliated by cracking Ley with a high stick. Then it was gloves off, and bedlam.

Before that, Pat Stapleton had shoved several inches of stick into the groin of Alexander Gusev. Gusev, riled and staggering, threw his stick at Dombrowski when he failed to call a penalty. The Canadians were particularly agitated by Dombrowski's peculiar call against MacGregor.

Canada was behind 3-2 at the time. The penalty completely frustrated the Canadians. The game was lost.

MacGregor, skating out of the Russian zone, was charged into the boards by Vasiljev. Dombrowski, on top of the play for once, threw up his arm to signify a minor penalty, presumably to Vasiljev. Vasiljev, gloves off, piled into the startled MacGregor. He struck the former New York Ranger five times in the head, the obvious aggressor, but not in the official's eyes. MacGregor tussled with his opponent, but did not take off his gloves. After peace was restored, Dombrowski tagged both players with five-minute penalties for fighting.

This was in total disregard for international hockey law, which calls for 10 minutes for the man who starts the fight. Dombrowski, in absolute confusion, forgot about the minor penalty to Vasiljev.

After the game, one Canadian had enough class to be dismayed at the rowdiness.

"There was no need for that kind of crap at the end," said Bobby Hull. "Of course, it was a lousy call against MacGregor."

But Hull refused to endorse any retaliation in the attitudes represented by Ley's quarrel with Kharlamov, by Marty Howe's shoving a linesman, by Stapleton's prodding a foe with six inches of lumber.

"Blow up and you only show how exasperated you are with the referee—or

66

with yourself."

While the players lost their cool on the ice, coach Billy Harris lost his cool that day at the practice session, sufficiently annoyed at Team Canada's banal practicing that he abandoned the exercise before it was finished.

Team Canada had gone through an hour of aimless passing and carefree shooting. Harris was on the ice too, though barely noticeable. He occasionally blew tentative whistles to signify line changes in a sloppy, no-contact scrimmage. Not once did he raise his voice. At last, obviously exasperated, Harris skated to the players' box and climbed inside. Then he raised his voice.

"Okay. If some of you goddamn guys want to go home today, that's fine with me."

Then he strode off to his dressing room, refusing to talk to reporters.

"Just describe what you saw."

The practice was rancid. Few seemed to care that Team Canada looked terrible in losing the fifth game to the Russians. For a team in trouble, the practice seemed to be a skylarking session for lesser players on the order of the laughing Paul Shmyr, the wise-cracking Paul Henderson, the joking Mike Walton.

Hull was asked for an opinion of Harris' stomping out of practice.

"He should have stomped a few guys off," Hull said, blunt as six inches of hockey stick driven into

(Top left) Bruce MacGregor makes his feelings plain to the referee.

(Left) Typical of action during tonight's game, one of many skirmishes.

(Top right) There was no question of whose side the Russian fans were on.

(Left) MacGregor wheels in front of the Russian goal to chase an errant pass.

(Bottom) Typical action in the Russian end. Four defenders tie up Backstrom and Howe.

(Right) Jim Harrison skates for a rebound. Tretiak has just made a brilliant save from the point.

your belly by Howe. "We've got too many slackers on this team."

So the day started badly and ended worse, from Harris leaving practice in disgust to Ley attempting to start a war all by himself. Even the Team Canada steering committee was in bad sorts, boycotting the game because of what they considered shoddy treatment at the hands of the Soviet officials. But somehow they managed to squeeze a hockey game in admist all the bitterness.

Only 34 seconds into the game, Mikhailov scored from the slot to net the Soviets an early lead. The Canadians must have been thinking about something

else. Marty Howe managed to pick up a minor penalty 20 seconds later, paving the way for a power play goal by Vasiljev, his third of the series. Gordie Howe and Houle managed to tie the score early in the second, but Anisin scored his first of the series to put the Russians ahead to stay by the time MacGregor and Vasiljev had their little set-to.

Canada's scoring was finished for the night, and the Soviets went on to get two more before the final bell to take the game 5-2, and a two game lead in the series.

Asked if he felt his team could come back and win the last two games and

salvage at least a tie in the series, Harris replied.

"We had to win tonight. It's hard to motivate players to win two games just to get a tie."

Henderson was ready to go home after the game. Bill Hunter was swearing at Dombrowski during the game for his incompetence. Billy Harris seemed to have given up before the game. The Canadian newspapers were all predicting an ice war in Game 7. In Canada, Our Side had the Russians on the run and let them get away. Here, the Russians have the Canadians on the run, and they're still running, straight into Game 7.

The start of it all. Cheevers skates over to the timekeeper
to check on the clock with 1:28 remaining in the game.

GAME SEVEN

CANADA 4—USSR 4

Line-ups

RUSSIA
Goal: Tretiak, Sidelinkov.
Defence: Gusev, Lutchenko, Vasiljev, Tsygankov, Tiurin, Shatalov.
Forwards: Kapustin, Maltsev, Lebedev, Mikhailov, Yakushev, Petrov, Kharlamov, Vikulov, Schadrin, Anisin, Bodunov, Kotov.

CANADA
Goal: Cheevers, Gratton.
Defence: Ley, Tremblay, Stapleton, Smith, Shmyr, Hamilton.
Forwards: Houle, Lacroix, Webster, Gordie Howe, Mark Howe, Backstrom, Harrison, Hull, Henderson, Benier, Tardif, McKenzie.

First Period

1. Russia, Anisin (Lutchenko) 3:34.
2. Russia, Tiurin (Lebedev, Yakushev) 6:47.
3. Canada, Webster (Lacroix) 17:42.

Penalties: None.

Second Period

4. Backstrom (G. Howe, Mark Howe) 2:55.
5. Mark Howe (Tremblay, Backstrom) 6:38.
6. Gusev (Petrov, Kharlamov) 7:20.
7. Mikhailov (Petrov, Kharlamov) 7:59.

Penalties: Lutchenko 6:11; Stapleton 7:06; Maltsev 9:18.

Third Period

8. Canada, Backstrom (Tremblay) 6:38.

Penalties: None.

Shots on goal

Canada	10	13	7—30
Russia	11	7	3—21

Paul Henderson, striking a pose similar to 1972, raises his stick to signal a goal by Hull. It didn't count, as the referee ruled time had expired.

October 5, Moscow

—Tom Brown is going to have a lot of explaining to do when he gets back to Toronto next week after the hockey series. Referee Brown was the goat in the Gardens on September 19th when he disallowed a goal by Petrov which would have put the Russians back in the game. Tonight, his call went against Canada. Had he allowed the goal in the final second of play which Hull had apparently scored, the Canadians would have walked off with a 5-4 squeaker and a chance to come out of the series with at least a tie. As it was, Canada and Russia played to a 4-4 draw, assuring Russia of a winning margin in the series.

Today's game was expected to be a bloodbath, a carry over from Game 6 in which Ley and Kharlamov engaged in a Ley-inspired post-game bout. Billy Harris was concerned about the violence, having cast his gentlemen athletes in the role of international diplomats and bearers of peace and good will. The players felt that they could maintain their cool, however, and with two Canadians officiating, at least get a better break than had been given them thus far in the series.

Canada could have tied the series up with wins today and tomorrow, and at least have gone home as non-losers, if not winners. But there must have been a general feeling of gloom across the country that Team Canada was going to lose today. Howe had been tied up too long by the Soviet Six to be really effective, and the Russians had been keeping the puck away from Bobby Hull very neatly and limiting his scoring chances.

Anisin and Tiurin had shot the Russians into an early lead. By 6:47 of the first period, it looked as if it was all over. The Russians didn't seem to be in any hurry to mount an offence until they had a three-man attack ready. Their puck control effectively stifled the Canadians. They were toying with the Canadians. They seemed sure of winning.

Tom Webster scored for Canada with 2:18 remaining in the first period. This seemed to bring new life to the Canadian side. Some of the chippiness of the 6th game was apparent, and the Canadians began to test Tretiak.

It's difficult to say that Tretiak had been lucky up to this point. However, the few good shots that the Canadians did have were labelled, and he came up with the big save time and time again. He had to have something besides skill to pull off with some of the saves he made in that first period. Tretiak stopped Tardiff, Backstrom and Harrison from close range, and Gordie Howe bounced a shot off the goal post with an open net yawning.

When you're hot, you're hot.

Number 17 for the Russians, Kharlamov, had an outstanding first period. Repeatedly he sifted through the Canadian team and fired on the net. Some of this luck around the goal was due to sloppy Canadian play; much of it was due to skill. In the first period the Russians were clearly outskating the Canadians, who still seemed to be having trouble with the extra 15 feet of ice surface. The Russians were taking full advantage of it. The Canadians seemed to be often confused with shots coming off the backboards.

Ralph Backstrom scored a stylish goal in the second to tie the game. At 6:38 of that period Mark Howe put the Canadians in the lead, but that was quickly erased a minute-and-a-half later when Gusev and Mikhailov scored. Both goals were scored within 39 seconds of each other. Play went from end to end during the period, with both teams missing good scoring opportunities. Gordie Howe missed his second open net, and some of the Canadian players seemed so intent on getting the puck to Hull that they passed up good shots which might have scored goals.

(Above) Gordie Howe. Nothing more needs to be said.

(Left) Valery Vasiljev, whom many felt to be the best Russian on the ice.

The second period may have been the best that Team Canada has played. The lack of heavy body checking seemed to help the Canadians regain their poise. Even Ley has played well. Roundly booed in the opening ceremony for today's game, Ley played as though the incident in Game 6 never happened. It seems that he wasn't afraid of retaliation, and indeed there was none.

Backstrom scored from Tremblay at 6:38 of the period, but only after the Canadians had exerted tremendous pressure around the Soviet net. Both McKenzie and Henderson missed shots that might have been goals.

Until 1:32 remained in the game (or 1:28, depending on which side of the rink you sit), Brown had called a fair game. It was obvious that both teams had heeded warnings from their respective officials to clean up their act. But then the roof fell in, just when Brown thought he might get out of the game with his scalp. As Brown said later, "It's the story of my life."

With 1:28 left on the clock play was stopped, and Cheevers ponderously rushed to the timekeeper's bench to complain about the clock. He had noticed that the clock had clicked on for three or four seconds after play had been halted. Brown checked on it, and told the timekeeper to allow two seconds to elapse before restarting the clock. This took considerable courage on the part of the Canadian referee. Not too many referees in any part of the world would have done this in front of the hostile crowd that faced him tonight. The Russians fans, naturally, roundly booed Brown for this action. You can bet that European referees who worked the three previous games here wouldn't have allowed the extra time.

Then, in the dying seconds, the Canadians stormed in one final fury to score, Cheevers replaced with a sixth attacker. drove the puck past There were only seconds left when Hull took a pass from Henderson and blasted the puck past Tretiak from a scramble in front of the net. The red light went on, indicating a goal, almost at the same time as the green showed to end the game. The goal was disallowed, the game was over, and the score remained tied, meaning that Canada couldn't possibly tie the series.

"I got the puck in the slot and let it go," said Hull. "I saw the puck go into the net and I looked up and saw the red light go on. I figured that was the game for us."

Brown claims that he didn't see the light go on, but in fact had seen the green light go on first to end the game.

Backstrom was bitter. "I asked the referee why he didn't allow the goal and he said he checked with the Russian linesman who told Brown that he had watched the clock run out. I don't know why he'd be watching the clock in that situation."

Apparently the goal light and the game light weren't synchronized as they are in Canada, so that didn't help. Also, for the first time in the series, the Russians weren't using the digital clock that records tenths of a second. In other words, it was a pure judgment call by the referee.

"We won that game 5-4 and that's it," said Cheevers. "We lost at least four seconds when they let the clock continue running after that whistle in the third and besides that, the red light went on and it couldn't flash if the green light was on."

Even Robert Ford, the Canadian ambassador, got into the act.

76

"I'm distressed," he said.

Alan Eagleson: "It's tough when they don't count the ones that go in."

The only one to agree with Brown publicly was Boris Kulagin. "I heard the referee blow the whistle and my players stopped to show their discipline."

Like hell.

(Left) Action around the Russian net.

(Below) The disallowed goal from another angle.

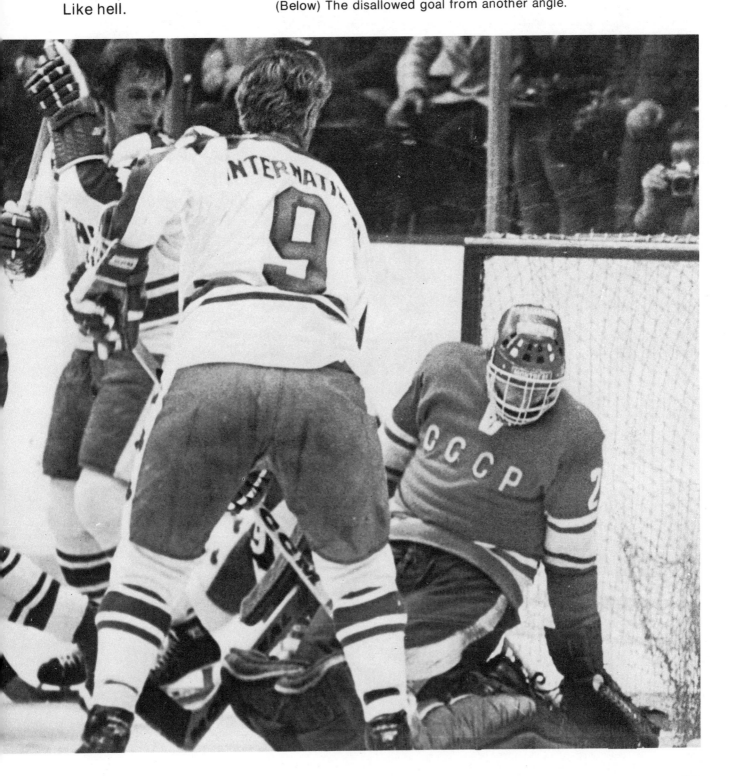

With less than two minutes to go in the game, Gordie
Howe sits in the penalty box, aware that it's all over.

GAME EIGHT

USSR 3—CANADA 2

Line-ups

CANADA
Goal: Cheevers, Gratton.
Defence: Ley, Tremblay, Stapleton, Selwood, Marty Howe, Hamilton.
Forwards: Houle, Lacroix, Webster, Gordie Howe, Mark Howe, Backstrom, Harrison, Hull, Bernier, Tardif, Mahovlich, Walton.

RUSSIA
Goal: Sidelinkov, Polupanov.
Defence: Gusev, Lutchenko, Vasiljev, Tiurin, Liapkin, Kuznetsov.
Forwards: Kapustin, Maltsev, Yakushev, Kharlamov, Vikulov, Schadrin, Anisin, Kotov, Shalimov, Popov.

First Period

1. Canada, Hull (Backstrom, Tremblay) 13:47.

Penalties: Webster 7:57, Yakushev 13:08, Tiurin 5:26, Hamilton 18:21.

Second Period

2. Russia, Yakushev (Schadrin) 6:27.

Penalties: Popov 2:18, Ley 2:18, Harrison 6:12, Harrison 10:34, Harrison 18:10, Marty Howe 19:03.

Third Period

3. Russia, Shalimov 0:53.
4. Russia, Shalimov (Yakushev) 6:59.
5. Canada, Backstrom (G. Howe, Ley) 12:42.

Penalties: Schadrin, Stapleton 2:15, G. Howe 7:50, Tiurin 19:20, Canada, 19:58.

Shots on goal

Canada	10	8	6—24
Russia	10	12	8—30

Ralph Backstrom scores Canada's second goal and the
last of the game in the third. Canada lost 3-2.

October 6, Moscow

—Before going into tonight's game Team Canada was down by two and couldn't possibly win. A win tonight would have at least closed the gap up a bit and made things respectable. As it was, Team Canada lost their last game on Soviet ice 3-2, and lost the series to the Russians by three games. Since the Russians figured that they had won the 1972 series on total goals, one can only wonder how they'll look at this one. In any case, the Russians won, and, in sum beat the Canadian team soundly. One bland radio announcer even went so far as to call the series a farce.

But if there were complications and confusion and bitterness and recriminations before this, tonight's game had to be the alpha and the omega of Russian cheek. The Soviet Ice Hockey Federation, under the guidance of Andre Starovoitov, sent a letter to Bill Hunter before the game stating that, should the Canadians revert to their dirty tactics of previous games, the Soviet team would be pulled off the ice.

This was a peculiar move, since the Canadians had incurred only two minor penalties the night before.

What made it even more peculiar was the fact that the announcement was made over the public address system to the crowd just as the Canadian team was warming up.

The Soviets accused the WHA team (all of a sudden they're not the Canadian team anymore) of breaking all the rules, of being the provocateurs and the ruffians. The Soviets had done nothing wrong.

This is one of the most amazing, if not most obnoxious, conditions ever laid out before an international competition. It had the effect of making the Canadian side very aware of even the most implied infraction on their part. Jim Harrison din't much care, though. He belted everyone in sight. The game was played to the Soviet standards from start to finish.

The fact that the Soviets indeed do nothing wrong was made very clear in the third period when Pat Stapleton was the victim of a stick attack by Vladimir Shadrin, which drew blood. When Stapleton saw that referee Kompalla was going to be slow in calling a penalty, if he was going to call one at all, the Team Canada defenceman rushed up to Kompalla and smeared some

(Right) Cheevers smothers as Shmyr protects the net.

(Below) Cheevers stickhandles as Hull stares in amazement.

blood on his cheek. Crude, but effective. Schadrin got the major, but Stapleton received a 10-minute misconduct for besmirching the referee.

Bill Hunter of Edmonton was not a happy man when he read the Soviet pronouncement:

"Taking into consideration the fact that the players of Team Canada 74 have repeatedly broken the agreement signed by the World Hockey Association and the USSR Ice Hockey Federation on adhering to the rules of the International Ice Hockey League, which was expressed by dirty play, appeals to the referee and spectators, the USSR Ice Hockey Federation states that such competitions in the spirit of the best traditions of sport and friendship, is forced, that at the first infringement of the above-mentioned agreement, to stop play of the last game."

Starovoitov's syntax was garbled, but his intent wasn't. He was pulling the old Soviet hockey ploy of bluffing an opponent. The Canadians did not call his bluff. The game was fast and fancy, as devoid of boisterous play as an uncommonly tame taffypull. Both teams abandoned body contact.

Hunter, red-haired and volatile, blew what passes for his stack.

"This is a sickening, sickening situation" he shouted at Starovoitov in the broad aisle separating the dressing rooms. "You have sunk to the lowest degree of sportsmanship in history. Who the hell do you people think you are? God?"

Starovoitov, surrounded by flunkies, moved away muttering what might have been, "The hell with Canutskies."

"And another thing," Hunter hollered after his departing foe. "If you pull your team off the ice, you'll never again play in international competition."

Mrs. Ben Hatskin, wife of the owner of Winnipeg Jets, soothed Hunter. "Don't let them upset you, Bill."

Hunter sounded as benign as anyone when expressing goodwill and fellowship. "These Soviets don't upset me, my dear. They sicken me."

Sickening, from a Canadian patriot's view, was the fact that the Canadian players did not check vigorously enough to make Starovoitov put up or shut up.

On top of it all, the pot was still boiling over the disallowed Canadian goal of the night before. It was announced yesterday that Canada was going to pack it in and take their hockey sticks home in protest over the disallowed goal. But Big Bill Hunter, after losing a protest to the Soviet Ice Hockey Federation over the goal, assembled the team and they unanimously agreed to play. They owed it to the fans here, both Soviet and Canadian, who came to see the game, and the fans at home. They also owed it to the telecast sponsors and the WHA. They won't pack too many paying customers into Edmonton or Vancouver to see a pack of quitters.

Had Team Canada been ahead in the series the story might have been somewhat different. But they weren't, and any action on their part had to be scrutinized. The sour gripes approach was out. It was bush. It was something associated with a second-rate team. And although Team WHA didn't win this one, there was no way they'd admit to being second rate.

The Russians "rested" five of their first stringers today, including the near-invincible Vladimir Tretiak. This is the first game in 16 international matches with Canada that Tretiak hasn't played. He came out of it all with a good record: 6 wins, 5 losses, and 4 ties over two years. The Russians also rested Tsygankov, Vasiljev, Petrov, and Mikhailhov, all prominent this year. They believed they had the series won, and indeed they had in light of the disallowed goal and disallowed protest over it from the night before. No matter what happened tonight, the Canadians were returning home as losers.

SUMMARY

FROM RUSSIA — WITH LOVE?

Luzhniki Arena, 20 minutes from the Kremlin in downtown Moscow, is a bright, well-lighted place, the hockey heart of the Soviet Union.

There, one morning, during the Great International Icecapade, was a chance to know a few of the Soviet Selects as people, rather than mere numbers in a program. Language barriers and their red helmets always make them seem more like robots than humans, the Bad Guys of hockey's Ice Age.

Bob Lewis of *Time* magazine's Toronto bureau had arranged for an interpreter, the tall, bald, urbane Felix Rosenthal, a Soviet citizen who works for *Time's* Moscow bureau. I was privileged to tailgate and ask a few questions of my own.

"Russian hockey differs from the Canadian pros in one major respect," Alexander Maltsev was saying through Rosenthal. "Every player gets to show his best in games between Soviet teams, because our less chippy play helps us show our best."
Maltsev is dark and stocky, 26 years removed from his birthplace in the Siberian town of Kiorv-Chepetsk, beyond the Urals. He wore, this day, a dark blue sweatsuit, not practicing because of a sore leg suffered the night before in a collision with energetic Rejean Houle.

Maltsev, on the ice, is always wheeling and turning, an elusive skater, seldom standing still, a career centre who played left wing in seven of the eight games against Team Canada. His abundant skills are reminiscent of a Henri Richard or David Keon, quick, smooth skaters who have been ornaments in the National League for a long time.

Vaclav Nedomansky and Richard Farda, prominent Czech players, fled through a chink in the Hockey Curtain last summer to sign with Toronto Toros for a mess of pottage. Maltsev was asked if he'd prefer to abandon his studies in electrical engineering for a chance to become instantly affluent in the WHA or NHL?

His response seemed careful, guarded, as though a Big Brother such as Chuckles Kulagin was listening.

"I would be very interested to see what it would be like to be part of an NHL club. To see how it's done and how it works. But the professional money does not appeal to me nearly as much as being part of our national championships. Our game is not so rough, so I can show all my skills."

For all his skills, the Soviet Ice Hockey Federation rewards Maltsev with a three-room apartment and a car, luxuries by the spartan standards of ordinary Soviet citizens. Maltsev's modest menagerie includes one pretty wife and one small daughter. His wife, Susanne, was an actress before their marriage.

Maltsev kept coming back to the robust Canadian fashion, with particular reference to the rambunctious John (Cowboy) McKenzie, who used to rope runaway calves at the Calgary Stampede.

"McKenzie," Maltsev said, "has a bad name in the Soviet Union."

The rangy Alexander Yakushev clumped off the ice, all whalebone and whipcord, perhaps the best left wing on the planet, at least no worse than 1-2-3 at the position dominated by Robert Marvin Hull.

Yakushev's father worked in an iron foundry, one of the many belching plants that pollute the Moscow sky. Alexander, or Sasha, learned to skate on ice in the courtyard below his parents' cramped apartment.

"My first idols," he said through the interpreter, "were Boris Mayorov and Antaoli Firsov. When I was growing, they were big in our game."

Yakushev gazed at Canadian reporters, small smile lines bracketing his mouth. "After this series," he said, "I have another hero. Bobby Hull, He is clean, and so very good."

Yakushev, training to become a physical education teacher, is the proprietor of one wife and one daughter. Canadian fans know his as Yak 15, his nickname and his number, entirely appropriate. The Russians have a plane called the YAK 15.

Yakushev turned to a Canadian photographer who had shot a picture of Yak 15 posing with Hull. "I would like very much," he said, "to have Hull sign it."

The request was subsequently relayed to Hull, whose availability to the press and the public made him the most popular Canadian in the Soviet Union.

"Of course I'll sign it," Hull said. "But on one condition. I want him to sign one for me."

Hull is burdened with making the Winnipeg Jets respectable, and he added, "If I could, what I'd really like Yakushev to do is sign a contract with Winnipeg. God, but he's good."

The reactions of Yakushev and Hull to each other, their mutual respect, relieved the hockey hysteria of the Super Bowlski. Stripped of all the politics and bitching, a series at the summit is right when two adversaries can genuinely say of each other, "He's damn good, and I like him."

Hull would say, on the eve of the first confrontation in Quebec City, "We are representing Canada as a free country and free citizens. We want to show people of other countries how much we appreciate living in a free country."

I yield to practically no one in my appreciation of Hull, but, one step removed from the hostilities, I could not share the notion that grave moral issues were at stake. Some of the semi-prose inflicted upon Canadian readers did imply that grave moral issues were at stake, that an ideological struggle was upon us, another twilight of civilization.

For me, in the beginning, it demanded a public confession of inadequacy: I am not omniscient enough to sit in moral judgment of any system or any people. I am only a sports writer hoping to report with reasonable accuracy who won and how it was done. The good ones in my business — one thinks immediately of Edward MacCabe of the Ottawa Journal, Scott Young of The Globe and Mail, and Red Fisher of the Montreal Star — would share such a disclaimer.

No matter how exciting the series, the good ones in the pressbox were aware that the fate of civilization turned on other hinges, that one billion Chinese will remain unaware of the final score.

Since Hull brought it up, however, what about the capitalistic system? Buy or die often appears to be its message. Those who buy the free-enterprise system escape massacre and economic ostracism, but our culture grows leprous with the absorption of cannibal values. Communism is not necessarily the only grinding form or repression.

On the other hand, the cultural revolution that Marxism entails can be an unbearable impoverishment, a forfeiting of the intellectual's most cherished heritage.

The exile of Alexander Solzhenitsyn or the bulldozer destruction of non-conformist art in Moscow two weeks before Team Canada arrived remind us of the appalling price the proletarian dictators must exact, in return for the least relief in the condition of the masses.

Capitalism is good, for Hull and the Howes and other Canadians lucky enough to become hockey royalists. Communism presumably is splendid, for Kharlamov and Yakushev and other Russians whose hockey precocity provide them with a better material existence than their Soviet contemporaries.

But when Hull unloads the big slapshot, or Howe reverts to the grandeur that was Gordie, or the nimble Kharlamov scoots around a baffled defenceman with the quick skittering of an aroused water beetle — that is the hard point of real joy.

There is no mistaking what is good, anywhere. When hockey is right it transcends the borders, the moralities, the bloody mistakes of the bureaucratic boobs who run the world everywhere.

And so Boris Mikhailov, this morning in Moscow: tough, implacable, the captain of the Soviet Selects, in many ways their collective soul. "That No. 13," the elder Howe had said of Mikhailov, "he is their spirit."

Mikhailov, caught in a clutch of Canadian writers after practice, said, for frank openers, "When Canadian hockey players fight, they spoil sport."

It was an unsubtle reference to Rick Ley's assault on Kharlamov after the siren wailed to signify completion of the sixth game.

"I was frustrated," Ley remarked afterward, "so I hit the first Russian closest to me."

The next day Ley had the grace to recant. He approached Kharlamov in Luzhniki and said, "I'm not mad at you. I was just mad at the bad officiating, so I apologize for taking it out on you."

Kharlamov, dark and unsmiling, gripped Ley's hand but did not say a word. The hatchet was buried, but in a shallow, well-marked grave.

Mikhailov continued his frank assessment of the Canadian urge to clobber. "I would not want to play in the NHL or WHA. There is too much dirty play. I prefer not to play for such a team."

But chippiness is a word cut to fit venial sins in any hockey language. It was Mikhailov, two years ago, who directed a vicious kick at the shins of Gary Bergman, a defensive hub for Team 72.

"Hull, Cheevers and Tremblay," Mikhailov said of three Team 74 hubs, "they are true sportsmen to be liked. Not dirty."

He is lean and dapper, with one of those Bob Hope noses that looks as though it has been dished in by a punch. He came to Moscow Lokmotiv of the Soviet Union's first division through the Labor Reserve Sports Club. He is the senior member of the Selects, 30 on Oct. 6, married to a nurse, father of one son who, at 7, is a goaltender.

"I hope to play a long time, like Howe," Mikhailov said. "Unlike Howe, because my boy is in goal, I will never play on the same line with him."

Most Russian players, off the ice, wear haberdashery that resembles shapeless stuff plucked off the rack in the bargain basement at Eaton's, or the Gum department store. Not Mikhailov. He was resplendent in a dark brown double-breasted sports jacket and light brown checked slacks. Somewhere, in some dollar store, he bought the duds to make him more than a claiming plater whenever the clothes horses are running.

Mikhailov was told that Howe considered him the soul of the Soviet side, and he deflected the compliment. "That's not for me to say. Those on the outside can see better."

From the inside, Mikahailov said, he saw that some boisterous members of Team 74 "wanted to hunt down Russians. Not Hull. He is a gentleman on the ice, with a great shot. Cheevers is the

best Canadian goalie I ever played against. Tremblay has my respect because he never infringes on the rules."

What about Howe, whose last hurrah gratified Canadians?

"I have," Mikhailov said, "heard and read much about Howe. He has highly developed skills, not all clean. It is amazing a man an still play at 46."

He could not resist candor. "But we cannot compare Howe to Hull. He is lower in our estimation ."

"Because he gets his elbows up and frequently gets a piece of an opponent ." I asked.

"Da, da," Boris Mikhailov said quickly.

Remember the name. We are going to see it again, probably as a future coach of the Borscht Belt brigades.

And recall a cameo from 1972, after Paul Henderson scored *that* goal in the last minute of the last game. Mikhailov, that night, turned away from the jubilant Canadians and skated toward the dejected Soviet bench. The number on back of his jersey looked huge. No. 13.

This time, in the last game, there was no Mikhailov or Tretiak or Petrov or Vasiljev or Tsygankov or Lebedev. They were given the night off, not required for a contest the Soviet intermediates won 3-2.

WITH LOVE, INDEED

Roughly 2,500 Canadians, many of them prepared to behave like Grey Cup yahoos, included several sports on the make in 1972. To be certain they wouldn't get shut out in a sexless socialist state, some of the sports imported girl friends.

The chaperones of Team 72 made certain the athletes would remain reasonably celibate in Moscow by flying over a shipment of the players' wives.

Harold Ballard, one of the 1972 chaperones, put it tastefully, as is his wont, "Our guys came to life when their wives arrived. The wives came with matresses strapped to their backs and our guys got the sex over with fast and went to work."

Raunchy Canadians under no marital regimentation discovered sexual delights, in 1972, easier to obtain than the the tourist manuals suggested. The Naughty Ninas were as forthright as Khrushchev when he hammered his shoe that time on a podium at the United Nations.

The press room for the 1972 visit was on the 20th floor of the Intourist Hotel, a modern flop known colloquially as the Moscow Hilton. On his first night in Moscow, one Canadian journalist was working at a typewriter next to an open window. The drapes were open.

The telephone rang and the reporter picked up the receiver. "Hello?"

"Hello," a woman's voice said. "You Canadian tourist who would like some fun?"

The reporter was surprised to hear a Russian speak such passable English, and the stirring in his loins suggested he would like some fun. Strange town, strange woman, but the same old notion.

Still, the bold call seemed peculiar. How did she know where to phone with her offer of commercial companionship?

"I live," she said, "in the apartment building right across from your hotel. You can come to my place, or I can come to your place."

The reporter, remembering all the warnings about Soviet traps, even sexual traps, decided to be prudent. Suppose she was bugged, in more ways than one? He thoughtfully passed the information along to another jockstrap journalist who, less discriminating, apparently made it with Irina.

A few yahoos, revealing a lamentable lack of toilet training, urinated in Red Square in 1972. Three exuberants from the self-important Ontario hamlet of Bolton expressed irreverence as they passed in line above old Lenin lying waxen in his tomb, resembling nothing so much as a refugee from Madame Tussaud's.

As the Bolton chaps peered at the remains of a bigger Soviet hero than Alexander Yakushev, one of them surreptitiously stuck a decal on the railing around the sacred tomb.

The decal, wonderfully smart-assed, advised, "COME TO BOLTON FOR OUR 1972 CENTENNIAL."

The 2,700 fans who

accompanied Team 74 were more genteel compared to their predecessors, most of them tourists first and hockey fans second, rather than the other way round. It was impossible for them to desecrate Red Square because the sprawling cobble-stoned plaza, the Russian equivalent of St. Peter's in Rome, was closed for repairs.

The 74 crowd was quieter than the noisy 72 mob, not one of them in danger of being arrested. Only one was apprehended in 1972, but he would have had considerable company if the Moscow cops had not been so long suffering. The Canadian lout arrested in 1972 smashed up a bar in the Intourist Hotel, then slugged two hotel security officers when they attemped to put him to bed.

Team 74's look at Moscow, as superficial as Team 72's, inspired unflattering critiques of the Soviet Union. Tour director Ben Hatskin, a Winnipeg rogue, and his vivacious wife Cecille were ensconced in the cramped clothes closet that masquerades as the royal suite in Rossiya Hotel. It is a massive flophouse, one block square, 3,200 rooms and 6,000 beds.

"By the time my wife got her clothes unpacked," the ample Mr. Hatskin reported, "there wasn't enough space left to shoehorn a cockroach into the room. So I moved my bed into the corridor and slept there."

Mr. Hatskin was overstating the cosy accommodations in the Rossiya, but perhaps not by much. Gordon Howe claimed he has been exposed to a worse hostelry, in Detroit, when he was a distinguished right wing with the Red Wings.

"The Shamrock in Detroit was lousier," Howe insisted. "The Shamrock had hot and cold running maids. I mean they were hot with the cold steel of a knife or a gun if you trifled with them, or left your wallet lying around loose."

In the Rossiya, Howe and his wife Colleen discovered their room was bugged. "I mean the bugs were running around the bathroom. Cockroaches, I believe."

Howe was relieved when a reporter told him that Cossack cockroaches are harmless compared to the cunning worms in Zaire, which bore holes through the soles of your shoes and wind up nesting in the bags beneath your eyeballs.

James Hunt, a prolonged radio jabbertiser from Toronto, is an old Moscow hand, an unquiet veteran of the fulsome coverage of Team 72.

"The Russian cockroaches aren't dangerous," Hunt told Howe. "And you can tell a Russian cockroach because they always wear fur hats with earflaps."

We are, as affluent Canadians, scornful observers wherever we face poverty, inefficiency, or dirt — all of which the Soviet Union has in abundance.

The moment we set well-shod feet abroad we forget that some of our cities have appalling slums, that our public transportation can be abominable, that we have many hotels which are the ultra deluxe in fleabags.

Instead, we compare the worst in Russia with the best in Canada: food, for example. Most Russian food seems nourishing, although heavy and rarely varied. There is excellent fodder in Montreal and Toronto but between Hamilton and Winnipeg, Regina and Saskatoon, Edmonton and Otter Haunch, B.C., is a gastronomic wasteland.

The food they do well in Moscow, the borscht and the black bread and sour cream, is a gourmet's delight. Chicken Kiev is a delicacy, a poultry treat that would water the mouth of even old chicken-fried Colonel Sanders.

Team 74 was chaperoned by Mr. Hatskin and Wild William Hunter of Edmonton, both of whom may have regretted the presence of the players' wives.

"This was a holiday series," Hunter would say. "Not a hockey series. Next time, if there is a next time for the WHA, there won't be any wives along."

Billy Harris at least partially agreed. "With our wives along," the coach said, "many of us were tourists on a second honeymoon."

Other Canadians, with no marital impediments, discovered the Naughty Ninas were as obliging as in 1972, if not more so. Testimony was offered by Bob Shortly, a 33-year-old unmarried accountant from Toronto.

"You can sort out the prosties and their pimps around the hotel bars," Shortly said. "The girls make a pitch for pantyhose when you strike up an acquaintance. Then they want you to buy a bottle of champagne to make whoopee. Then they suggest 20 rubles as the starting price for an assignation."

At the Russian rip-off rate of about one rube for $1.30 Canadian, the price per assignation is roughly $25.

Shortly found out that the comradeship of the comradely cuties does not extend to liasons in hotel rooms. "It's always their place, not yours. The cops don't hassle them in the lobbies, but you have to make love at their place. Their place is frequently the kitchen of their parents' three-room apartment."

Shortly also noticed how inflation has hit the pin-trading game. "Used to be you could get a colored badge with Lenin's ugly kisser on it for one piece of bubble gum. Now you have to give three wads of gum for one badge."

The ubiquitous Hull was the busiest Canadian trader. He imported a sack full of Canadian geegaws imprinted with the Canadian flag and other true-north-strong-and-free trinkets. Every day, after the Canadians finished practice, he used up an hour swapping pins and signing autographs. He charmed Moscow.

One day Hull tried to trade one Canadian pin, even up, for one friendly Muscovite's gold front tooth, but the gentleman said "nyet."

Hull left Moscow with a sack full of Russian gadgets and junk. "When I get home," he said, "I'm going to open my own hardware store in Hamiota, Man."

The 2,700 Team Canada

tourists represented more Canadians than we've ever shipped overseas in one chauvinistic lot, outside of a World War. Most experienced, for the first time, the strange, foreign conditions of downtown Russia, drawn toward that silent mother who can devour.

It was difficult to realize, caught up in the shinny excitement in the benign sunshine of a Soviet October, that out there, beyond the broad city limits, is a boundless ocean of a country that tormented Napoleon and Hitler in their vain attempts to conquer Moscow.

The casual visitor, contemplating the brooding mustard-colored Kremlin walls, could only report the small adventures of Canadian travellers. There was not enough time to grasp the suffering soul of Russia, because a lifetime might not be enough time.

Russian youth seems to be reaching for Western notions, sometimes literally trampled as they grasp. One morning J.C. Tremblay strolled out of Luzhniki Arena, followed by hordes of small boys seeking to exchange cheap Soviet badges for chewing gum.

Tremblay ambled to back of the team bus and opened a window. As the bus pulled away from the arena, he threw handfuls of gum to the scrambling boys. They fought for sticks of the coveted confection on the asphalt yard. One kid, on his hands and knees, got his hand crushed under the heel of a policeman's boot. The others ran away with their gummy goodies.

Russians who disdain gum are right, of course: children who chew it, as Canadian parents know, are frequently the dentist's best customers. The sugar content creates juvenile cavities. Russian parents claim they don't want their offspring soliciting from strangers for another reason. "Please don't corrupt our youth by offering them things," a Moscow woman named Leda warned a Canadian. "We don't want them begging."

There is almost universal conviction that all hotel rooms are tapped, as well as many apartments. Visitors sometimes arrive with paper and pencil, communicating by writing while they carry on banter directed toward the bug, which may be in the ashtray, or the light, or behind the picture on the wall.

If there are such bugs, the obedient Reds obliged to transcribe such messages are going to be hips deep in vulgar speeches from Canadians who began each morning by declaring to the bug, "Now see here, you no-good, leftist Commie freak..."

Many could not wait to retreat from Moscow, but only one defected before the series finished. Dennis Murphy, the WHA president, which involves being a spear-carrier for Hatskin, deserted Team 74 after the sixth game, protesting "shoddy treatment" by the Soviet Ice Hockey Federation. "Too many cockroaches, too many bad seats in the rinks, too much bad refereeing. That's why I'm leaving."

The whiners included Louis Lefaive, chairman of the International Committee of Hockey Canada, an Ottawa civil servant who, according to Hockey Canada president Douglas Fisher, can take credit for a large part of the arrangements for a 74 Summit.

And Lefaive did write, in Team 74's official program, in part: "...These kind of exchanges between great hockey teams should become a natural and normal part of the continuing development of hockey as a sport...and of the friendly relationships that should exist between the nations taking part."

It seemed peculiar, then, that Lefaive would join other tour officials in boycotting one of the games, refusing to attend because he did not have an adequate view in Luzhniki.

If Lefaive deserves the credit Fisher awards him, then he must accept the possibility of being given some seats in dark corners, in getting rob jobs from some referees, including Canadian referees, in being bivouacked in hotels not on a par with first-rate Canadian accommodation.

Lefaive and everybody else connected with Team 74's alleged goodwill mission to Moscow knew last summer that the inept Victor Dombrowski of the Soviet Union would referee two of the eight games. They knew, from previous experience, they might have to accept rooming with the odd cockroach as part of agreements with the sly Soviets. They should know that the Russians can casually break any promise as though it was never made.

The time to complain was last summer, before the committments for the series were complete. If Team 74's promoters were suspicious of a Russian doublecross, they should have abandoned the series in July. To whine after the fact is to deserve the most crushing term in the vocabulary of sports. The term is bush.

CHAMPAGNE WENT FLAT

There had been an exhibition game in Czechoslovakia against the Czech nationals, and Team 74 lost 3-1, and the next morning there was a takeoff for Toronto through pale-Prague sunlight.

The champagne flight went flat over Greenland, the airborne liquor cabinet finally empty, everybody slightly sozzled to take the sting from certain memories.

The WHA's European excursion was finished and there was nothing left, in the nine-hour return to Toronto, except to recap for The Globe & Mail while the party was getting a glow on.

The simple assessment is that, head to head with the Soviets and the Czechs, we only have a chance to regain our hockey dominance by sending our best — with the hope that they'll play their best. With scant exceptions — Howe, Cheevers, Stapleton, Hull and notably Ralph Backstrom — Team 74 did not qualify as our best. They did not, as a pertinent example, have any centres to match the Phil Esposito and Bobby Clarke of Team 72. When Espo and Clarke walked in the dressing room

door in that other memorable September, complacency flew out the window.

Cheevers in goal for Team 74 was superior to either Ken Dryden or Tony Esposito for Team 72. Backstrom, at 37, weaved more skilful skating patterns than he has for five years, justifiably chosen as the classiest Canadian in the last two Moscow games. The underrated Stapleton, deft with the puck, solid against fancy forwards, is among the best rearguards on earth.

Although he did not exhibit it in Moscow, Hull is our supershooter of all the years. In Moscow, Hull was shadowed by two Russians whenever he got near the puck, which was seldom because his centre, Andre Lacroix, spent more time spearing than he did passing.

If a combined NHL-WHA team is dispatched against the Soviets in 1976, Hull may need an Act of Parliament to be selected. His impeccable good manners made him popular on Gorki Street, as they do on any street anywhere, but he is not R. Alan Eagleson's favorite pin-up player. The boss of the NHL Players Association, who is attempting to organize a 1976 super series, detests Hull from another picture.

"You can bet I'll do everything possible to keep Hull off," R. Alan announced, not quietly, in the cavernous lobby of the Rossiya after the last game.

"That's not a smart thing to say," said Red Fisher of the Montreal Star, who was listening.

Lacroix, animated and expressive, told French Canadian press attaches,

"You guys really missed a story when we were in Finland. When it comes out, you'll know why we lost."

"It concerns Bobby Hull," one WHA owner said, requesting anonyminity, after a third drink. "Some of the players are really down on him, if you can believe it."

It can be believed. Many mercenaries, jealous in their well-earned inferiority to Hull, on and off the ice, insist Hull is only for himself, that his sense of public relations is so much show and sham.

Only bushers would utter such claptrap. If Hull's ceaseless catering to the public is good for himself, it is also good for everybody connected with the game. He elevates the pygmies. If he had not given the WHA a shred of respectability, by abandoning the NHL, many of his detractors would be back in the Bush Leagues.

The WHA owners have collectively blown an estimated $25-million in the past two seasons and Hull, aware that every WHA player loses if the league folds, is an owners' man. That throws him into confrontation with the union biggies, Eagleson in the NHL, Ronald Roberts in the WHA.

The WHA owner confided, "Hull is arguing against the exorbitant demands of the unions because the demands could force some of us into bankruptcy. He recognizes that the owners have got to make something if the players are to make anything. A lot of this came to a head on this trip. The nice guy got shafted by several of the rank-and-file clerks and it bothered him. The Howes are with him, but you'd be surprised how many on this trip weren't."

Hull's response to the rumors of dissension was typical. "Only a handful gave us trouble. If they'd pulled their weight we could have been more respectable."

Respectable? Pulling weight? Ah, there, Gordon Howe, No. 9, 47 next March 31, a monument to anybody who cares about Canadian hockey. Howe went back 15 years for some of what everybody thought he'd lost in the never-stopping tomorrows of 26 seasons.

The abundance of Howe kept rolling up, accretions of memory, skills of the buffeting years. His themes are great ones: a boy's child-play, a man's life, the gladitorial fight with time.

I have the best of possible jobs, cutting small words to fit large muscles, for a newspaper I respect, trying to say something about the human condition every day, in language as polished as the demands of deadline will allow. Emotionally, I long ago moved over to the middle-aged side of the room, and I root for mature judgment when pitted against the outrageous fortunes of chronology. It is a broad stroke of irony that if the Team 74 players with youth on their side had responded to the challenges as Howe did, Team 74 would have won the Super Bowlski.

The rare ones like Howe jeer at the years, and there is no other like Howe. He went through his patriotic exercises with a defiance that makes you appreciate what he is: an old hockey player going through the pantomine of youth, pretending it's still natural.

"God, I'm tired," he told Bill Hunter, in the letdown of losing.

But in Hockey Night in Minsk, for all the wrangling and disputes, Howe summoned up enough to take us all back to a time when we were all a lot younger.